THE WAY Y

THROUGH THE EYES OF A CHILD

Tobogganing down a tussocky, icy slope on a tin tray with just a sodden woollen gym-slip between you and the snow was an unforgettable experience...

THE warmth of the bakery wall glowed through my hand-knitted jumper and skirt as we made ourselves as tall as we could so that none of the bakehouse heat was wasted.

Every evening at dusk, we village children would gather together there in our 'gang'; eventually we would trudge home reluctantly before the bogeyman came to get us.

Mr Dibble the baker had long since gone home. His horse had been stabled for the night and we could hear her snuffling around in her narrow stable.

The strong smell of the horse and the sweet smell of hay blended strangely with the dusty flour that covered the cracked bricks of the old bakery walls.

"When the Nazis come, they're going to kill us, send us away to Germany and live in our houses - especially the vicar's!"

We gazed in horror at the speaker. Acker, the leader of our gang at the age of ten, was the oldest and wisest among us. If anyone knew what was in store for us, he did, or so we thought.

It is strange that after all the years that have passed, I can still recall the warmth of that wall and the immediate feeling of terror generated by the conversation.

At the age of six, to be alive in the Monmouthshire countryside was bliss - too young to miss the taste of bananas, receptive to the flavours of dried eggs and Spam, and revelling in every wonderful day and the experiences that came with it - wartime Britain was the only place to be.

It may seem odd in these uncertain times, when children have to be supervised more carefully, that a little girl of six, nicely brought up by loving parents, should be allowed to play outside in a secluded country lane in the twilight, without being watched over by an adult.

All children then could wander at will through our village, take picnics to the bluebell wood, and stay out for hours, without a word being said.

If you were thirsty you could knock on anyone's door and ask for a cup of water. It was never refused.

A grazed knee would be bandaged and cuts and bruises doused with horrid, stinging iodine at any house in the village. Politeness was the key word.

There was only one person whose door we would not knock on - Mrs Saxby's.

We all knew that the old lady was a witch, just waiting to cast a spell on anyone bold enough to approach that dark-green blistered and bubbly front door.

Mrs Saxby was a widow with a small, hunched body and without a tooth in her head. She also had two large and ugly ginger tom cats. She smelled and they smelled, and we would cross the street with our fingers crossed for luck rather than pass her overgrown front garden.

On the other side of the street was the local pub. During the week it was a quiet place, with the local men using it during the evenings, but on a Sunday it became extremely busy with visitors from Wales - to avoid the licensing law there, they would travel over the border into England for a pint.

During these war years the pace of life seemed to slow down rather than speed up.

The shortage of petrol for motoring brought out the horses and carts for local travel and deliveries.

It was my delight on a Saturday morning to help Mr Jones the milkman with his round. Sitting up on the wooden bench seat behind Ben the horse, holding the thick leather reins, I felt like a princess. Ben was a working horse; he smelt strongly and always appeared to be moulting.

The countryside is not always idyllic.

We lived in a rented non-insulated Victorian house that was bitterly cold in winter. Ice formed beautiful patterns inside the window frames, and getting out of bed was a classic manoeuvre.

*Travel and trade in the country once relied on horsepower
(or in this case donkey-power)!*

We leapt from one rug to another, trying to avoid the icy-cold floor boards. Even the contents of the chamber pot were sometimes found to be frozen!

Our outside lavatory was kept spotlessly clean and regularly white-washed, but during the autumn months huge spiders used to stand out starkly against the outside walls.

The loo was tastefully concealed in laurel bushes and honey-suckle and I used to love the peace of the place in summertime - you could hear bees and insects buzzing around outside.

Wartime lighting restrictions meant that having to go to the lavatory at night was difficult. A small torch had to be held downwards so as not to attract enemy planes.

No adult accompanied us - it was considered cowardly to be afraid of the dark. Anyway, what was out there to harm us?

Our proximity to industrial south Wales and Bristol often led to air-raid warnings.

Our air-raid shelter was in the orchard and was half buried underground. Our next-door neighbours shared it with us - they had one of their own but it was very damp (with true country common sense, they had flooded theirs and kept ducks in it).

We enjoyed their company when the siren went, and relished the ducks at Christmas during those difficult years.

School was of passing interest to me. The male teachers had vanished into the armed forces, and the elderly ladies who took their place were kind, firm and undemanding. The frequent threat of air-raids made each day exciting but did little for us academically.

When the siren went, we all lined up at the classroom door and ran home to our own shelters as fast as possible, our gas mask holders banging against our hips as we ran.

If there was no all-clear hooter before 1.30pm we were free for the rest of the day. I spent many minutes praying for a reprieve from the awful music lessons which seemed to take up most school afternoons.

I have not checked up on statistics, but I feel sure that the weather was colder in the winters then but warmer during the war-time summers.

Tobogganing down over tussocky, icy grass slopes on a tin tray with only a sodden, semi-frozen woollen gym-slip between you and the grass was an unforgettable experience.

The warm, heady perfumed days of summer with scarlet poppies and blue cornflowers growing in the meadow grasses seemed to last forever. In some fields down by the river the grasses came over our heads, and we lived in a world of our own.

Toys were hard to come by, so we had to amuse ourselves. The pace of life was slow and people were simpler and more gentle.

I feel eternally grateful for the village life that I led in wartime Britain when I was a child.

- Pam Clatworthy

There were only two bedrooms in our bungalow; us five boys all slept in one bed - three at one end and two at the other...

I WAS born in a small village in Hampshire called Ewshott. The main Ewshott village was about a mile away and our part consisted of ten houses and bungalows, with two farms.

I was the youngest of five boys, and there were only about ten other children in our part of the village.

My aunt and uncle owned one of the farms, and I remember my aunt churning the butter in the dairy to make cheese.

There were only two bedrooms in our bungalow and us five boys all slept in one bed - three at one end and two at the other. Our water well was a few yards from the scullery entrance door, and when it was dry my brothers and I had to walk to a well at the bottom of a neighbour's garden.

The surrounding area was nearly all military ground, and common land and woods covered by the gamekeeper Mr Giles - Farmer Giles to us. Primroses, bluebells and violets were abundant in the woods and the common land, as were snakes. They were mainly adders and we avoided them if at all possible.

Our school was nearly two miles away in Crondal, and the school supplied us with a bowl of soup and a piece of bread in the winter months, and a cup of cocoa with a slice of cake in the summer.

There were no buses, and most adults rode a bike and did their shopping in Farnham or Aldershot, about four or five miles away.

I liked living there, but when I was nearly seven my father got a job in Essex and we had to move. We had to say goodbye to all our friends and relatives, although I have visited a lot over the years.

The memories of my happy time living there still remain with me nearly 70 years on.

- Reginald Cox

6

We ate our sandwiches and played roly-polies down the grassy slopes...

I WAS born in Leyton and my school was in a scheme which organised annual choral concerts of massed school choirs at the Crystal Palace.

I longed to go to the Crystal Palace - it sounded just like fairyland - but only the school choir was allowed to go.

To get into the choir you had to pass a simple sight reading test taken by the headmistress. I tried again and again and again to pass my test - how that poor woman must have dreaded the footsteps on the little wooden stair and the timid knock on the door!

Then one day she sighed and said, "I think that will have to do".

My heart sank, I thought she was trying to say, "You've had more than enough chances, please don't bother me again".

But no, the dear, kind lady handed me my certificate, signed Miss Emily Dell. I was in the choir!

So we practised all the songs. There was Danny Boy, The Meeting of the Waters and The Faery Song from The Immortal Hour - all lovely tunes and very pleasing words which were nice and easy to remember.

The concert conductor paid a visit to every school to give a few words of advice and a quick rehearsal. I can't remember his name, but I do recall that he lived in Arundel Gardens in some strange, faraway place called Goodmayes, Ilford.

At long last the great day came.

The concert hall held several thousand children and the singing must have sounded wonderful.

Each block of seats had a different coloured programme and we were all told to take along a large white handkerchief.

When the signals were given, we had to wave or flap these up or down or round and round and it made quite a pretty effect. Our mums must have been very proud of us.

We didn't pay much attention to the building itself. No one told us that it was a great feat of civil engineering and that it had once stood in Hyde Park and housed the Great Exhibition of 1851.

The building at Sydenham stood on a slight rise with sloping lawns all round.

We ate our sandwiches and spent the rest of lunchtime playing roly-polies down the grassy slopes. We *deserved* to be sick!

I must go back and see if the grassy slopes are still as inviting...

- Ivy Ball

There were ballads, like Young Lochinvar, but best of all was Hiawatha, which lasted a whole term...

MISS Machell came to our school twice a week, to teach art and needlework. Art with Miss Machell meant copying from cards she brought with her - prints of flowers, fruit or sunny meadows; needlework was lazy-daisy, stem stitch and french knots applied to tray cloths or duchess sets supplied at parents' expense.

At the end of the hour Miss Machell praised neat work extravagantly and - fortunately for me - was too kind-hearted to do more than sigh over anything careless or messy.

This was in the 1930s, and you may well wonder why I look back and remember Miss Machell with gratitude. She certainly didn't teach me to draw or to sew, which was presumably what she was paid to do. She did something better - she read aloud to the class as we worked.

She always read poetry, but poetry with a story that held our interest and a rhythm like music. There were ballads, like Young Lochinvar, but best of all was Hiawatha which lasted a whole term and which I read for myself as soon as the holidays came.

Thank you, Miss Machell, for showing me that poetry was for pleasure, and not something to be gabbled off to prove we'd learnt it for homework.

- Irene Howlett

My friend and I wore Mickey and Minnie Mouse costumes and were invited to shake hands with the children coming out...

MY FIRST memory of treading the boards was when I was five. It was at Margate and I was invited on stage to sing 'I Do Like A Dumpling In A Stewedle-oodle-ooh'. I was given a bag of sweets for my effort.

I was born in 1921 but only just scraped into the world, a very poor little mite. Yet I escaped all the childhood illnesses my sisters had, so I must have been a tough little cookie.

Joining the local dancing class, Molly Lynn's Linnets, opened up a whole new world for me.

Then we progressed to the Rhythm Babes and toured the northern towns in variety and pantomime. At twelve years old I was going to school in each different town.

Tea Time Cabaret at Dickens and Jones in London was a great time. My friend and I wore Mickey and Minnie Mouse costumes. When a Walt Disney film was showing at the Leicester Square Theatre, we were invited to shake hands with the children coming out. Sitting in the taxi coming back in our costumes we really felt we had made it.

But the best was yet to come, when we did the Moss Empire circuit. We were on the bill with Nat Gonella at the Shepherds Bush Empire, Sophie Tucker at the Hackney Empire, panto and variety at Chiswick - oh happy days!

Mum's ambition was for me to be a Tiller Girl. As I never grew taller that four foot nothing there was no chance of that!

How fortunate I feel for having had such a happy childhood.

- Lillian Thirkell

*Grace was a walkie-talkie,
my Christmas gift the year my brother
got his big red motor. With nylon hair
you could style, she was so
aloof in manner and looks,
sophisticated rather than cuddly...*

WHEN I peered into the window of the recently-opened 'Antiques & Collectables' shop in the high street, the sign which caught my eye sent the clock whizzing back about forty-five years!

Black letters on white background and with a red cross in the centre, read 'Dolls Hospital'.

Margaret was a Christmas present. A large, life-like, second-hand doll, with a china head and big blue eyes that closed, she caused many stares, lying in my mother's lap, then tucked beneath her arm as she walked from the bus.

Day in, day out, there Margaret would be, propped up against the doll's cot, nursing sick toys, wearing one of my father's large handkerchiefs for her nurse's cap.

Then, one day, she fell backwards - maybe tired from her never-ending duties! - cracking her head on my bedroom lino. The blue eyes fell in and her skull cracked.

I was inconsolable. So off we went to the nearest 'Dolls Hospital' and in a few days, she was home again, right as rain.

About five years later, as I walked towards Margaret, who sat on a chair by the bed, I saw her lean forwards as if in slow-motion and fall headlong to the floor, before I could reach her to catch her.

This time, not only was I shattered, but my doll's china head was too.

11

The crown was now beyond repair, the eyes gone again.

We didn't live near the hospital any more, so my father painstakingly rebuilt her head, with layer upon layer of bandage soaked in glue. From then on, she always wore hats - but I wish I could recall what became of her, when I grew up!

Then there were Daphne and Golly and Peggy, who was a small black doll, dressed in orange and white-knitted clothes. As a small girl reluctant to go to the bathroom, I discovered her sitting on the closed toilet seat when, finally, I gave in!

But Betty was my doctor's favourite. Made of celluloid, her pale complexion always led him to comment on her ill-health, while he let me spin around in his surgery chair.

Grace was a walkie-talkie, my Christmas gift the year my younger brother got his 'big red motor'. With nylon hair you could style, she was sophisticated rather than cuddly, aloof in manner and in looks.

And there were the miniature ration books, bought with precious pennies at the shop near the roundabout in Eltham, just across the road and down a bit from the chemist, where saved-up three-penny bits bought a 'Teddy' hot-water bottle - with a little help from my mother.

I also had two traditional bears, one golden-furred called Teddy, the other a deeper brown I called Bobby.

I was too young to remember when they arrived, but they saw me through thick and thin did my bears.

As their pads wore out, and their seams grew loose, I would put them to sleep with a pin-prick in the arm, before anaesthetising them, with a tea-spoon over nose and mouth.

This had happened to me, at six years old, in what was then the Eltham Cottage Hospital, when I went in for a tonsils and adenoids operation, the fashionable cure at that time for constant colds!

The bears, once 'asleep', would be repaired by a childish hand, then left to recover, watched over by the nurse, Margaret.

They were passed to my brother, as I grew up and what became of them I don't know. He certainly doesn't have them now, 45 years later. But then, I have the memories, haven't I, brought back by signs, like the one in the high street shop window.

- Barbara Johnson

We would run straight into the pantry and grab home-made bread and fronds of rock semper...

THE majority of my childhood was spent on a smallholding in the remote village of Sunk Island on the Humber coast. In fact my youngest brother still carries on the farm, which is all Crown land.

We had a wonderful time. Our school holidays were spent playing in the rock pools on the Humber coast, and we collected rock semper (samphire) by the bucketful. This Mum washed, boiled and steeped in vinegar. It was delicious - full of iron!

I can taste it now. We would run home from school, run straight into the pantry, grab chunks of home-made bread and at the same time pinch the fronds of rock semper, sucking it off the stalk.

There was only one weekly bus to Hull to begin with, then this increased to two a week. I only went to the pictures two or three times up to the age of fourteen. At fifteen I was a maid at various farms, earning eight shillings a week.

Then I began nursing and did five years training. Despite the Blitz on Hull it was a wonderful life.

On my day off I would catch the bus from Hull to Patrington, collect my bike from my grandma's and pedal the three miles home to Sunk Island.

The girls I trained with were educated at Hull Grammar, whereas I was educated at the village school.

When the girls told me that there were a hundred pupils in their school, and asked how many were in mine I said fourteen. But I didn't enlighten them when they thought I meant fourteen hundred!

Nursing was hard work with long hours, but whether it was the iron from the rock semper, or the fact that with having only eight years schooling I had to work twice as hard as the others, I became an SRN in 1948, and a midwife in 1951.

I could write reams about those years. All the happiness and sorrow of nursing, the wartime casualties, getting locked out after lights out, the times we fell in and out of love and the pranks played by the doctors...

- Pat Farr

A wounded crewman from the
Heinkel was heard to say:
"For you soon the big lick".
George said with a wry smile:
"He means the invasion is coming and
we are going to get a good licking"...

I T WAS August 17, 1940. In those days boys never walked, they always ran, and we were not fortunate enough to own cycles - this was a privilege reserved for adults.

Mickey and I had been running up a chalk farm track on the summit of the South Downs, north of Worthing.

Turning right, and leaving the track, we found ourselves in chest-high grass and hawthorn bushes. There was a strange smell of pear drops and vinegar.

We pushed through some brambles, and there it was - a German Heinkel III bomber!

It had crash-landed the day before, wheels up, sliding on its belly for half a mile. It had finally come to rest on the rim of a chalk pit.

George was telling the story of the battle to a small crowd of onlookers. Two years older than us with a large smile and freckles, he was big for his age, and was wise far beyond his years.

He was more than willing to tell his story again for our benefit. He had been doing his farm chores when the aircraft had crashed, and when he arrived at the scene the wounded were being treated, and the Captain was being interrogated.

According to George, the Captain had started to give instructions to the police and the Home Guard, but was curtly informed: "Prisoners of war do not give orders, they take them".

A wounded crewman, waiting to go for hospital treatment, was heard to say, "For you soon the big lick".

The onlooker had been puzzled by this, but George knew what he was trying to convey.

"He means the invasion is coming, and we are going to get a good licking," said George, with a wry smile as we gazed at the parachute packs and the equipment laid out on the ground.

A crashed Heinkel bomber with its knobs and levers was paradise for curious schoolboys. It drew them like a magnet...

The great dark green bullet-riddled monster was full of menace, strange and forbidding even in defeat.

Mick and I followed George around the wing, past the oil-soaked engine and twisted propeller blades, to the nose compartment.

It was huge. Constructed in clear plastic, like a great curved greenhouse. Inside there were more buttons, knobs and levers than I had seen in all of my ten years.

Entering the aircraft through a side hatch we picked our way gingerly through a discarded pile of flying equipment. It was stifling, the summer sun had made the aluminium sides too hot to touch.

Climbing into the pilot's seat I stared out over the chalk pit. By pushing the rudder pedals I could hear the huge tail section moving at the rear. I tried to visualise the traumatic circumstances of the previous day but it was all to much for a country lad of my age.

Stepping out through the hatch the three of us examined the tail. I remember Mickey looking up at the insignia and exclaiming, "A swotiska!".

George gave him a friendly shove, "Swastika, stupid".

It drew us children like a magnet.

Hardly a day went by that we did not visit the wreck. I unscrewed instruments and took them home. I had no idea what their function might be, but the luminous dials looked beautiful in the darkness of my bedroom.

On one occasion Mickey was undoing a nut on a cylinder and a hissing noise ensued. Somebody shouted 'Poison gas!', and we ran away like startled rabbits.

George was shaking with mirth. "It's an oxygen bottle, stupid," he said. We were shaking too, but not with mirth.

Later in the week three R A F personnel arrived. They proceeded to remove the tail - for a trophy I guessed. The officer smiled and nodded in our direction. His arm was in a sling. I was impressed. "He didn't shoot it down," said George. "He hasn't got any wings on his tunic".

The next major item to vanish was a propeller blade - sawn off overnight. Almost a year later a chap called Peter handed it in for scrap.

One day, however, we went to see it and the plane had gone. George ambled off, giving us a wave before he strode out of sight, and from our vantage point, high on the Downs, we could look far out to sea.

"There's the big lick," I said, surveying the sparkling water of the English Channel.

"I see no invasion," Mickey replied, laughing.

- *Shaun French*

The cinema manager nabbed us.
He had been puzzled by the fact that one
person had gone into the ladies and
sixteen had come out, four of them boys...

EVERYONE was poor in our neighbourhood and the closest I ever came to affluence was the day I fell into the canal. I was carried to a nearby house - and what a house! It had carpets on the floor, lampshades, and a telephone (I had never even seen a telephone before).

I was driven home in the gardener's van - another first; I had never been in a vehicle that was not owned by the Corporation or the railway. It was a wonderful day... until I saw my mother's face.

My mother was always bright red up to her elbows; now the redness had spread to her face.

She was livid. "Your shoes are ruined, your jumper's shrunk!" she screamed at me.

I remember trying to hide the brown muddy stains on my frock as if it would make a difference. When the man who had brought me home told her I had nearly drowned, I felt sure that mum would be more sympathetic.

If money, or I should say the lack of money, was a problem to my mother, it was never a problem to me. There were many ways to make some cash - running errands, scrubbing steps and brushing yards.

Taking rags to the rag man was a good little earner and damping them down a bit to make them weigh more added a few pence. Jam jars were worth four a penny and plenty could be earned returning lemonade and milk bottles.

Neighbours became used to me knocking on their doors asking for jam jars, rags, and bottles and were very kind to me. I have always found people with the least to give are far more generous than those who have more than enough.

One Saturday I discovered an amazing way to get rich quick without any effort. It came to me in a flash when I visited the toilets in the Astoria picture house.

I had paid sixpence to get in to see the morning matinee, and there in the ladies' toilets was a huge metal door with an exit sign above.

White painted block capitals said 'PUSH BAR TO OPEN' so I did. Daylight flooded in. Bells jangled in my head and cogs began turning fourteen to the dozen.

The following Saturday I told a select number of friends to wait outside the door with threepence entry fee. I then paid my sixpence, went to the ladies' and admitted seven children.

They got in for half price, I pocketed what I thought was a fortune and everyone was happy.

These children spread the word and pretty soon I was on my way to making my first pound.

Then the bubble burst. Two weeks before Christmas as we all came trundling out of the ladies, a very irate cinema manager nabbed us.

He was puzzled by the fact that one person had gone into the ladies and sixteen had come out, four of them boys.

As he marched me home by the scruff of the neck I began to wish I had never been fished out of that dirty, muddy canal!

- Sandra Johnson

We looked forward to settling in at Kirkmuirhill... coal had to be brought from the bunker, the range lit and the huge flock mattresses set to air in front of it while we rooted in the chest for bed linen...

SOME years ago when we were holidaying in Lanarkshire we stopped for a short time at Kirkmuirhill to pay a nostalgic visit to the village.

I wanted to show my children the place that held so many happy childhood memories for me, but alas the motorway had taken over, and with it had gone a number of local landmarks.

Today's city dwellers who feel the need to get away from it all set off for more distant places but when I was a girl such holidays were out of the question.

On the whole, holidays to us as children meant Kirkmuirhill, far enough out then to be in the country and sufficiently near, so that my father could travel back and forth by train each day to his work in Glasgow.

Looking back now I wonder at my mother's happy acceptance of this yearly exchange from housekeeping in our comparatively modern home to the primitive conditions of our little, two-roomed 'place'.

There was no doubt she was content to be among friends she had known since she had holidayed there as a child, and I suspect that she found it pleasant to be away from the anonymity of our Glasgow suburb.

Certainly, to my sister Nellie and I it had all the charm of adventure, and even the hard work of settling in was looked forward to... coal to be brought in from the outside bunker, the old-fashioned range lit and the huge flock mattresses set to air in front of it while we rooted through the bow-fronted chest of drawers to find bed linen and the thick waffle-patterned cotton covers for the wall beds.

We were then given a list and sent to the Co-operative store for supplies, with just a little extra money so that we could stop at the little 'jenny a things' shop on the way home and buy liquorice strips, tablet and be allowed to tap out squares of toffee with Miss B's rubber hammer from the tray.

Meanwhile mother, with father's help, brought in water from the outside tap. We did have the luxury of an outside W C but all water for washing and cooking had to be carried in, no small chore on the first day when, after its winter disuse, everything had to be scrubbed clean, in particular the kitchen table. There were no tablecloths here, just heavy, sensible cutlery and equally heavy ironstone pottery.

Meals were a very special part of our holiday. Mother, never a great cook, bought large boiling fowls and cooked them gently on the range, accompanied by a fine assortment of vegetables, lentils and pearl barley.

On the first day succulent pieces of chicken, finished off by frying in butter, arrived on our plates, together with small new potatoes and other vegetables. Next day we had delicious soup, followed by cold chicken and crisp salads.

Time was never an important factor. Boiled rice slowly came to its best, enlivened by the addition of raspberries or maybe blaeberries gathered by my sister and I. Although we picked eagerly, many of the berries never reached the dish; we came home with blue stained mouths and fingers that told their own tale!

We had a griddle that swung over the hottest part of the fire, on which any frying was done. Just occasionally mother made drop scones on this.

One could buy bread, fish and other foods easily and a girl from the farm came round daily with fresh eggs and milk. And on the few occasions when we ran short of milk, Nellie and I set off to the farm with our small churn to collect it.

The farm goat we had to pass was tethered but had a nasty gleam in his eye and I was totally convinced that if he put his mind to it he could get free and attack us!

It was not all work. From the moment of waking in our sloping wall bed until the long, lamplit evenings playing ludo or card games, our days were filled with interest.

I suppose now one would think very carefully before allowing young girls the freedom we enjoyed, but somehow the fact that

Jeannie and a holiday companion at Kirkmuirhill

there were gypsies in a semi-permanent encampment in the glen at the foot of the village worried neither our parents or those of our friends.

Nothing can take from me the sheer remembered pleasure of guddling for baggaminies. I lay very still on the bank enjoying both the hot sun on my back and the coolness of the water under my hand as I held it very steady to catch one of the tiny fish, carried proudly in a jam jar. Sadly the poor things never quite survived long enough to be taken back to Glasgow in spite of our tender care.

Childhood memory is notoriously selective, discarding the dull parts and remembering the more interesting.

While I can now recall the excitement of sitting in the window seat during a summer storm and watching the lightning zig-zagging over the hills and listening for the next clap of thunder, in retrospect the days were all warm. I can never remember a rainy washday!

Quite an event this, starting early by lighting the fire under the brick boiler in the communal washhouse, filling it up with water and putting the clothes in, wringing them out in the mangle, rinsing in cold water and putting them through the mangle again until they were ready to be hung out in the hot sun (no easy-care materials then).

Our midday meal on washday was necessarily a hasty one so that mother could spread an old blanket on the ever-accommodating table and get on with the mammoth ironing that followed.

She had to make do with a 'fillet' iron, and to my horror I now see these featured among antiques! The shaped body of the casing had one of the two fillets inserted into the container while the other heated up in the glowing heart of the fire.

Weekends with father at home were very special, with trips to Lanark and ices in the Italian ice-cream parlour, choosing our favourite flavour from their large selection.

Saturdays were highlights, too, because that was a social occasion, with friends from further afield joining us, and to a certain extent we learned to depend on the frequent breakdowns of sound and picture so that we could walk round exchanging sweets and catching up on news.

I don't believe any later visit to the cinema has ever meant quite the same to me. In truth life was much simpler between the wars; it could be that we did not expect so much and were satisfied with what came our way!

- *Jeannie Peck*

F♀R KING AND COUNTRY

He suddenly felt very cold and found that there was a gap between his helmet and goggles and that the damp air from the clouds had frozen on his forehead. His fingers were numb but luckily were still capable of movement...

FROM my earliest years I remember how glamorous my eldest brother appeared to me. He was twelve years my senior and was at Cranwell. When he passed out as a pilot, I was immensely proud and took a photo of him back to school. He even came down there once and took me, with my best friend, out to tea, and I can still recall my disappointment that he did not come in uniform.

Later when the Second World War began I joined the WAAFs and it was in the RAF that I met my husband - another pilot.

We were rather thrilled while clearing out some old papers to find an essay, written in 1930, by my brother, when he was a Pilot Officer stationed at Duxford, with No 19 (Fighter) Squadron. The title puzzled us. 'Paid By The Day'. (Surely no RAF officer was paid daily!)

My brother, Flying Officer Roger Teale, described a day in winter when there was ten degrees of frost and a sprinkling of snow.

He was woken at 7.30am by his batman, took the Colour Hoisting duty at 8.30, after which it was bacon and eggs in the Mess before reporting to his Flight Commander, to see what was planned for the day.

Roger had to take a Sgt James and a Sgt Pearson on a battle flight. This consisted of climbing up to 16,000 feet and remaining up there for an hour and a half - not a pleasant task in a plane with an open cockpit.

Flying kit was donned - a Sidcot suit and sheepskin thigh boots, a scarf, leather helmet and goggles and three pairs of gloves, one over the other, the innermost pair being silk.

These gloves were still in existence some 20 years later and I used to wear them under another pair of gloves, when we were farming. The leather helmet was fur-lined, and my husband wore it for years when riding a motor bike, or in bitter weather when tractor driving. It is still in one of our drawers upstairs!

Finally, Roger strapped on his parachute, no doubt thinking that he was glad the awful training jumps were all behind him.

Then maps were collected. Three pencils were sharpened and tied to him with string, and a note pad was strapped to his right knee.

Outside the three engines were being warmed up, and were then left to idle, while the pilots made a final inspection and signed the inspection book.

"We will take off in formation," Roger told his two sergeants, "climb towards London and when I signal" (by waggling his wings) "you can break formation and stunt about, that is if it's clear up there. Keep near me and reform on signal.

Turning a machine over was the safest way to crash down, it seems, when things went terribly wrong

"We will land in formation and for the love of Mike, stick to me like glue in the clouds."

The three were ready in their aeroplanes. "Switch is off, petrol on, suck in." The mechanic repeated this and slowly turned the propeller

around, finally leaving it on compression.

"All clear. Contact, Sir," he called, and the pilot switched on and turned the handle of the starting magneto.

After a few backfires the engine started. Slowly it was opened to full speed, and if it sounded all right, it was checked with the revolution counter. Throttling back the engine, the altimeter was set and the pilot strapped himself in and waited for his companions.

When all three were ready, chocks were waved away and they tailed out to get into formation for take-off.

They hit cloud at 2,000 feet and it appeared to extend for miles and looked like snow clouds. They climbed as fast as possible and were soon in the cloudbank.

Roger checked that his companions were as close as possible, and set his course for 90 degrees with an airspeed of 65 mph which was the best climbing speed for the Siskins they were flying.

It was extremely cold but after what seemed an eternity they emerged into bright sunlight at 6,500 feet. Below the white cloud-tops gleamed in the sun, with dark valleys between edged with pink. Beautiful they might be, but they were blotting out the ground, and Roger just hoped that he was somewhere over London.

He suddenly felt very cold and found that there was a gap between his helmet and goggles and that the damp air from the clouds had frozen on his forehead. His fingers were numb but luckily were still capable of movement... they were just terribly painful.

At last the altimeter showed 16,000 feet and the signal was given to break formation, and Roger did a loop by way of a start. Then he chased the other two pilots and they all ended up having a dog-fight.

On the signal they re-formed and dived down vertically until they reached the clouds where they flattened out.

Suddenly the clouds thinned, and London appeared below. They flew round it on the windward side, in case one of the three engines failed.

"Pull off" parachute jumping from a Vickers Vimy

Then they went lower and turned for home at about 2,000 feet.

Presently the low cloud forced them down to under 100 feet and they indulged in the highly dangerous but amusing pastime of 'hedge-hopping', the extreme in low flying, much enjoyed by young pilots, and absolutely forbidden without an adequate excuse.

By the time the aerodrome was sighted it was snowing so after they flew over the camp, nice and low, to wake up the ground crews, they broke formation and landed independently.

It was comparatively hot in the flight office and Roger was helped out of his flying kit and warmed up with a hot whisky.

After lunch Roger was asked to go out again, this time with the Flight Commander, to practise aerobatics in formation. This was the first time that they'd done this routine and it was not too good so after half an hour they broke formation and Roger spun down from 5,000 feet. He disliked spins but remarked that the sooner he made himself like them, the better.

On return they watched some of the new pilots practising circuits and landings.

One pilot approached far too slowly and stalled just before touching down. The aircraft hit the ground and ballooned up to somersault and landed on its back. They ran to help the pilot get clear. He wasn't hurt (turning a machine over was the safest form of crashing down, it seems). "He won't come in that slowly again, I bet," Roger remarked.

Then routine inspections were completed, and the flight returned to the Mess for a hasty tea. There was the sound of people starting up cars, loading up luggage and giving final instructions to batmen about the care of their dogs during the weekend.

In half an hour the exodus was over, and those who were not free to leave camp, settled down to papers, sleep or a state of boredom, called 'doing nothing'.

"Another wonderful day," the essay concludes.

Reading this sixty years later, we suddenly realised that perhaps the young pilot writing all those years ago considered that each day paid *him*, in satisfaction and excitement, for his day's work in the RAF. Cash didn't come into it at all.

Sadly we shall never know, as Roger was killed just a few weeks later, while practising formation aerobatics for a display.

- Margaret Mason

We used to shout to members of the LDV, "Look, Duck and Vanish!" It often resulted in a clip round the ear...

I WAS 11 when Hitler's bombers began their onslaught against Britain. I lived with my mum, dad and younger brother in Sidcup, Kent.

One fine summer morning we were watching dad make ready to depart for Home Guard duty.

The Home Guard at that time had not been issued with a full uniform. I recall that they wore only a steel helmet and carried gas masks and rifles. Indeed at that time they had not even been awarded the title of Home Guard.

They wore a khaki armband with the letters LDV emblazoned in black upon it. This stood for Local Defence Volunteers but I remember that we used to shout after them, "LDV - Look, Duck and Vanish". This resulted in many wild chases, yelled threats and the occasional clip round the ear.

As my father reached the gate that morning the sudden sound of aeroplane engines cut short our family banter. A bomber appeared low, just above the roof tops, coming from London.

Smoke belched thickly from one engine. It was a Dornier, crippled and making a last desperate effort to get home.

My father leapt from his bicycle, rapidly loaded his rifle and opened fire on the enemy bomber. After each shot a flow of invective poured from his lips as he worked the bolt to eject the spent cartridge case and drive the next round into the breech.

The local policeman rode up and angrily demanded to know what he thought he was doing.

"Shooting bloody Huns, mate," my father shouted back. "Just like I was on the Somme in 1916."

And in the midst of this scenario of a flaming bomber, of rifle fire, the wailing of the air raid siren and the sound of our fighter planes approaching at high speed, my dear mother had but only one thought on her mind.

"Father!" she said "stop that foul language in front of those boys! Stop it this instant!"

- Don Fisher

I N THE war, how we all rallied round, from teenagers to the very old, doing our bit to keep our homes safe! We were living near an aerodrome and as soon as 'Wailing Willy' went off, we retreated underground. But one night in particular I shall never forget.

Apart from doodlebugs and incendiary bombs, everything was quite normal and we sat in the Anderson playing cards until, that is, we heard the 'secret weapon'.

There was a most peculiar sound, like nothing we had ever heard before. Dad climbed on top of the shelter as the 'swishing' noise got louder.

"For goodness sake, Tom" said my mother, "come back inside, it must be gas".

Some night that was! Falling bricks, wind in the trees, and this strange whooshing sound that went on all the time. We stayed inside, sleepless, as wardens in gas masks blew whistles and gesticulated wildly.

In the morning we found that a barrage balloon had broken loose, picked up a telegraph pole and, swinging it like a pendulum, had caused chaos.

Tiles, gutters, chimney stacks, greenhouses, fences and trees, all had suffered from this gigantic implement.

Secret weapons? Who needed them!

But were those wardens' faces red!

- Pearl Andrews

Three times a day the miscreant was required to report. He was given a tin mug filled with a concoction of vinegar, garlic, metal polish and other unidentifiable, evil-tasting ingredients...

ROYAL Naval punishments have traditionally been harsh. The cat-o'-nine-tails would break even the hardest of men. Very few survived keelhauling, and thieves would lose their fingers.

All punishments were administered in front of the assembled ship's company, with the captain witnessing the scene. This practice served the double purpose of deterrent and humiliation.

Humiliation seems to have been a tradition even where no punishment was involved.

We all know the time-worn phrases employed by senior rates ("You broke your mother's heart, you won't break mine", "Why should England tremble?", "A mother's gift to a nation" etc) as part of the initial 'breaking-in' of recruits.

The more draconian punishments have mercifully passed into oblivion, but the insistence on humiliation still lingers. Even today, the more serious punishments are accompanied by maximum publicity.

The guilty man is paraded in front of the ship's company for a warrant to be read out. There is a command 'Off cap!', but he is not even allowed to remove his own cap, this act being performed by the Master-at-Arms or Coxswain, who stands behind him

During training as a boy telegraphist at H M S 'Ganges' in 1951, I was put on a charge by my instructor for swearing at another boy.

Expecting that I would be dealt with by my Divisional Officer, I was surprised to be passed upwards through First Lieutenant's report, Commander's, and finally to Captain's report, which was usually reserved for the most serious charges, such as stealing, absconding, etc.

Trembling with apprehension, I listened to the stern admonishment from the mighty man, spoke my piece ("Yes, Sir."), and was sentenced to 14 days 'Gargle Routine'.

Now this was something entirely unknown to me, and I left the Captain's desk wondering what on earth was in store. I was soon to be enlightened.

Humiliation. Complete, abject, shameful, mortifying humiliation! No quick, sharp infliction of pain, not even fourteen consecutive doses, but the continuous, public parading of my utter disgrace!

Firstly, a gas-mask had to be worn at all times when not actually in one's own mess. In boys' training all activities were carried out 'at the double', so simply breathing is an effort, speaking intelligibly was almost impossible - and try to imagine sitting in front of a typewriter wearing headphones over a gas-mask, attempting to read morse with 100 per cent accuracy!

In addition, work had to be performed during the evenings, usually cleaning some compound or working in the galley, always wearing the gas-mask.

One hour each evening was spent doubling round a small parade-ground, carrying a broom-handle above the head - again, a difficult exercise made more difficult while breathing through the mask.

The ultimate in humiliation, however, was achieved by the

HMS Ganges, where young sailors learned the hard way. The weapon? Humiliation

All pals together. Even the 'gargle' punishment could not cure the swearing among young sailors

dreaded 'gargle'.

Three times a day, the miscreant was required to report to the Regulating Office, where he was given a tin mug filled with a concoction of vinegar, garlic, metal-polish and other unidentifiable, foul-smelling, evil-tasting ingredients. Accompanied by a Regulating Petty Officer, he would be marched onto the quarter-deck, where the following routine would be carried out 'by numbers'.

On the command 'One', the mug was raised high, and the boy shouted in a loud voice, "Ahoy, Ahoy, Ahoy! - this will make me a clean-mouthed boy."

'Two' - A mouthful was taken from the mug.

'Three' - Gargle.

'Four' - Spit out.

This routine, repeated until the mug was empty, encouraged the boy to take the largest mouthfuls he could manage, in order to reduce the number of repeats.

Ah, but now came the opportunity for the Regulating Petty Officer to indulge any sadistic trait (and sadism seemed to be a prerequisite for entry into the Regulating Branch) by pausing after

'Two' and 'Three' to see how well the boy could hold his breath and refrain from swallowing the obnoxious brew.

During 14 days of this treatment, three times daily, I was fortunate, but only once, to encounter an R P O with compassion enough to shorten the proceedings by ordering one shout ("Ahoy, etc...") and then in a kindly voice saying, "Throw it away, son".

I wonder whether that man ever realised how grateful I was for that small mercy!

Of course, this punishment stopped neither me nor any of the other boys from swearing, and I don't remember serving on any ship which was free from swearing, but I certainly thought up a few brand-new expletives to describe the instructor who charged me, and the Captain who ordered the 'Fourteen days gargle routine'!

- *Walter Anthony*

"The left hand side of the road has gone... on the right are people at a gate, laughing, crying and cuddling one another..."

WHEN I joined the WAAF I was posted to No. 1 Balloon Centre, Kidbrook, SE London. I was highly delighted as, living in Bow, I could get home on 24-hour passes.

One Saturday, my friend Audrey was going home with me. I had sweet-talked a shopkeeper into selling me a box of my mum's favourite Black Magic chocolates.

Waiting for a bus to take us through the Blackwall Tunnel, we saw a dogfight going on up above us. Young and exuberant, we cheered our boys on, little knowing what horrifying experience was in front of us.

I was looking forward to seeing mum, dad and younger brother Derek, but before we entered the tunnel, an air-raid siren sounded and we had to get off the bus and go into a shelter like an underground cavern, dirty, smelly and damp. Many people were there, including small, crying children.

After half an hour I started handing round mum's chocolates.

I stood at the shelter door for a crafty smoke and saw that everywhere was bright red. I thought, "Oh, God I'm dead and I have gone to hell". Fire engine bells were ringing and there were bangs, I would never see my beloved family again.

At about 5am the all-clear siren went and we got a lift in a ten tonner through the tunnel. That was as far as we could go. We just stood there, burning rubble all around, smoke, debris, pools of water. The East India Docks were completely gone. AFS and air-raid wardens were everywhere, and told us we could get to Bow, four miles away, only by 'Shanks Pony'.

Dirty and tired, we walked through bombed East India Dock Road, the most heart-breaking sight I had seen.

Finally we got to the corner of my street. The corner shop had gone. I turned my back and said to Audrey, "I can't look, tell me what you see."

"The left-hand side of the road has gone," she answered, "on the

right are a crowd of people at a gate, laughing, crying and cuddling one another."

I turned around, tears streaming, and a shout went up. "She's here, there's my Wynne!" My mum, dad, Derek, aunts, uncles and my little gran, were all running down the street, arms outstretched. We were all together for a few brief hours.

Dad had hung a huge Union Jack from the top of the house. There wasn't a window or door intact, but Derek, with typical Cockney humour, had chalked 'Window Cleaner Wanted'.

Our shoe soles had bubbled through walking over burning pavements. Dad repaired them before we returned to camp. That was the first of many similar nights of the Blitz - a night I will never forget.

- Wynne Ledger

RELATIONS REVISITED

"Let's escape with some of the fun fund," said Auntie C and we would board the bus, buying sugared almonds to eat in the Gaumont Cinema while watching Jessie Matthews dancing...

THE depression and recession of the Thirties scarred the spirits of many of my female relatives, but Auntie C was different.

Auntie C was fun - flambouyant, theatrical and musical. She started each day with optimism and song.

Wielding a strong tortoise-shell comb, she vigorously wetted her hair every morning with a mixture of sugar and water and then curled thick strands of it round flat metal pins. A pretty frilled mob-cap covered this sculptured arrangement as she went about her morning chores.

At midday, when all the saucepans and dishes had been scoured and dried and her menfolk sent out to the fields to toil, Auntie C would fill the flower-patterned wash-bowl. The mob-cap was then removed and her dried stiffened hair brushed and teased into an elaboration of fluffy curls.

Her soft, cushioned body was encased in pin-tucked, frilled or flowery frocks; her feet slid into high-heeled bar-

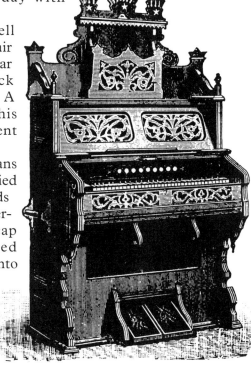

strapped shoes. She smelled of Attar of Roses.

Auntie C had a career. Every afternoon she endeavoured to pass on her exquisite musical prowess to visiting pupils, while seated on the tapestry-covered stool drawn up to the upright piano or the mirrored, ivory-stopped organ.

The money she earned was deposited in a shiny black box. She called it her 'fun fund'.

"Let's escape with some of the fun fund," she would say, and we would board the bus to our nearest town, buying sugared almonds to eat in the Gaumont Cinema while we watched Jessie Mathews dancing.

Sometimes, we had tea in the oak-panelled cafe which overlooked a square where the statue of Sister Dora Patterson stood in sentinel guard over the public lavatories.

And Aunty C made up stories about our fellow diners, they of the fox fur-clad shoulders, or veil-hatted arrogance, smoking cigarettes held in long, ornate holders.

"Let's keep our adventure a secret," she would say as we giggled our way back home; and there she would sit, straight-faced and sober, relating to her loved ones the problems of shopping in town and bemoaning the fact that the music shop was out of stock of music-tutor books, so that another visit there must be made very soon - turning her large grey eyes in my direction.

Every Sunday evening Auntie C played the organ at the Methodist Chapel.

This huge instrument of polished inlaid mahogany and gilded pipes was undaunting to her as her dainty feet peddled and her strong square hands darted about the stoppered plug board.

While the Bible-bashing preachers held forth in the 'long sermon', Auntie C and I hid behind the organ screen and played noughts and crosses.

She was a wonderful woman who livened up my childhood no end.

- Brenda Taylor

Travelling half-way round the world in those days was still a hazardous affair and it was with some trepidation that we watched father disappear...

IT WAS 1951 and my parents were managing a fish and chip shop plus a greengrocers in a small mining community in the Midlands.

They worked from the crack of dawn until well past midnight, every day except Sundays.

My father set out at first light to buy fresh produce from the Dukeries market gardens. He often took me with him in the school holidays and I loved wandering through the massive greenhouses, with their wonderful steamy atmospheres smelling of freshly-ripened tomatoes and cucumbers. But there was no time to linger.

Back at the shop, there were potatoes waiting to be 'rumbled', fish to be cleaned and filleted, crates of pop (including my favourite, dandelion and burdock) to be carried in and arranged on the shelves (often the night silence was shattered by one of these exploding pop bottles!).

Then the chip pans had to be cleaned and stoked ready for the lunch-time trade - oh yes, they were still coal-fired.

Meanwhile my mother was manning the greengrocers next door, boiling mussels or whelks, which she sold as a sideline, and coping with her domestic chores as well.

I was conscious even then of my mother being worn out by the end of the week. So my father made it a rule that, weather permitting, we would get away into the countryside on Sundays.

The only perk of the job was that he had the use of a Bradford Jowett 'shooting brake'.

It had no seats in the back so I perched on a banana box, but the back came down to make a super picnic table. We were not allowed to exceed 30 mph but then we were never in a hurry on Sundays.

My parents received the princely sum of £7 15s for their joint labours, which totalled well over two hundred hours a week, but we lived rent free.

Dad on the steps of the hut he shared with three other workers

Mum and Dad reunited. They are outside the new 'home' in Australia

As a child, I was not conscious of their financial struggle but I do remember overhearing my father asking for a pay rise and being refused. He was angry and short-tempered after that for a long time and there were muttered conversations between him and my mother which stopped abruptly when I appeared on the scene.

I knew something was about to happen. But it still came as a shock when my parents announced that we were going to emigrate to Australia!

There followed a series of visits to Australia House in London and to strange doctors for medical examinations. I thought all this activity wonderfully exciting and my school friends were very envious.

What I hadn't realised was that my father would have to go ahead of us, prepare somewhere for us to live, and then arrange for us to join him.

He was a bricklayer by trade and was contracted to work for the Australian Iron and Steel Company at Port Kembla in New South Wales. My parents had only to find the ten pound passage fee each and I would travel free. We had to agree to stay there for two years or pay back the full cost of the trip.

Eventually, everything was settled and my father was given his sailing date. He'd travel on the P&O Chitral out of Tilbury.

My parents had given notice at the shop and, incidentally, been offered the pay rise that had sparked off the move. My mother and I moved temporarily to a caravan in a local farmer's field to await our turn to board a liner for a new land.

We didn't travel down to the docks with my father but said our tearful farewells at the railway station in Nottingham.

Travelling half-way round the world in those days was still a hazardous affair and it was with some trepidation that we watched my father disappear from view. We never guessed that it would be over a year before we would see him again!

Postcards arrived at regular intervals from exotic places around the world and my teachers encouraged us all to search out these

The ship Dad sailed away on. The photo is a postcard from him which bore the messa

40

ports in our atlases. The journey to Sydney took four weeks and was considered a fast crossing. Interspersed with the postcards were our first pale blue air-mail letters which we thought most peculiar. I remember feeling very important when I first bought one at the post office to write to my father.

Along with most other 'migrant' workers, my father had been allocated a place in a hostel which resembled the POW camps we had grown used to during the war. I think it came as something of a shock to my father but he never complained in his letters. At least the weather was wonderful.

It was assumed that he would only be there for a short time until other accommodation became available but there was little private accommodation for rent and what there was seemed worse than the

pe you are being a good girl and getting all your homework done without much trouble"

hostel. My father decided to try to save enough money to buy a building plot and start building his own home. Many people bought land with a 'garage' erected on site and lived in the garage while building their home. There were no mortgages available or bank loans and I remember that my father had to save the princely sum of £350 to buy a building plot 100 yards by 50 yards with a wooden garage on site.

Eventually, he improved the 'garage' by adding a brick extension to provide a living/kitchen area and two small partitioned bedrooms. The toilet was at the bottom of the hill!

This, of course, all took time and money but at last he had what passed as a home for us and we were able to book a passage. Again, there was a delay while we waited for a ship.

After waiting almost a year, we had a passage, sailing from Tilbury, and the whole family accompanied us to the dockside for a tearful farewell. My mother promised to come back to see my grandmother as soon as possible but they never saw one another again.

The journey took seven weeks. Our ship, like so many migrant ships, proved to be barely seaworthy and we were twice reported lost at sea in storms.

We did eventually limp to port but my father went through a very harrowing time.

One year and two months after saying farewell on Nottingham station, my mother and I were reunited with my father, amid clouds of streamers and Scottish pipe bands, at Sydney docks in the pouring rain.

- Ann Jones

Once you went in, all aspects of domesticity and order vanished. A cousin swore he would not put his hat down in case a cat gave birth in it, and in the kitchen drawer was an incubator containing eggs at various stages of development...

A S A child, I suffered from travel sickness so that if I made a journey lasting longer than about ten minutes I usually arrived in an unsocially smelly condition.

A visit to the Green Street relatives involved two trams so it called for a great deal of concentration.

However, despite this initial ordeal, meeting my uncle, aunt and three girl cousins was an exciting prospect. Once you went through their front door all aspects of domesticity and order vanished.

They owned a music shop which contained three or four pianos surrounded by assorted musical instruments and gramophones. On wall shelves were stacks of sheet music, records and smaller items such as mouth organs, Jews' harps, tambourines and gramophone needles.

Order was unheard of.

My aunt had come from a well-heeled and somewhat eccentric family and had never been required to do anything beyond fulfilling her artistic trends.

Leading out of the shop was a 'kitchen-cum-office', though I'm certain no records were kept there. Again chaos reigned as boxes of 'fancy dresses' - the work of my aunt and any other member of the family who wished to contribute - were stacked in every alcove.

I was allowed to try on any garment which happened to be my size. Fancy-dress parties for young children were fairly common and I could be confident of winning a prize in one of my aunt's costumes.

Throughout the house, including the shop, was an all-pervading odour of cats which littered the place.

My first words on arrival were usually, "Have you any new kittens?", the answer being entirely predictable. Another cousin, in the Navy, swore he would never put his uniform hat down in case a cat gave birth in it!

To leave the ground floor you had to pass through a sort of closet where my aunt developed photographs.

She would show us films developing in trays of brown liquid, which seemed to us like pure magic.

I realise now that the contents of this room were positively lethal, for dotted around were sundry bowls of liquids which included ready-mixed permanganate of potash "in case anyone wanted to darken their skin if wearing an Eastern or gypsy costume". I never discovered the method of removal!

A door opened onto a yard that had the appearance of an ecological disaster.

This was uncle's province (when he wasn't selling or mending all things musical). There were three well-stocked chicken runs and he took great pride in the results.

In the kitchen there was an incubator with several drawers which, at certain times of the year, contained eggs at various stages of development and sometimes even chirping chicks.

With the exception of Christmas, when grandmother officiated, I don't recall ever eating a proper meal but eggs featured very prominently on the menu!

If a pudding was requested, uncle would send one of the girls next door to the confectioners for some rich cakes and ice creams. These were consumed on any flat surface not covered with a half-finished painting or heaps of sequins and beads.

Everything in the main room was large and heavy, the centrepiece being a long, solid table, which came into its own during family Christmas gatherings. When all signs of the feasting were removed, we would play games such as table tennis and blow football.

Taking up most of the wall was an overburdened sideboard which held bottles of home-made wine which exploded from time to time, creating a rather special aroma.

The chimney piece, flanked by shelves of photographs and general bric-a-brac, was overhung by a sagging mantelpiece. A fire always smouldered in the grate, fed by excessively large logs which jutted dangerously into the fender. This and the unguarded paraffin stove which heated the 'office', must have been an enormous fire hazard.

One Christmas activity perpetuated by my grandmother was a rollicking performance of Sir Roger de Coverley. This entailed dismantling the table leaving a space large enough for the dancers and the pianist.

As the dance progressed, the floor bounced up and down. This terrified me, as I was convinced that, at any moment, we would all go through to the cellar!

Uncle was a big-hearted, pipe-smoking man with a rather naughty sense of humour. His innocent tales were often interlaced with little ditties which my mother would have classed as 'not suitable for the children'.

He had no idea of money management, but it always seemed to be miraculously there. He sent his daughters to a local private school, but their attendance seemed to depend on whether they could get up on time.

Their haphazard education was compensated by the fact that each of them was unusually talented.

I loved uncle dearly, as I did my aunt - a plumply beautiful woman who did not seem to know the meaning of the word anxiety. Anything that struck her as comical would reduce her to a shaking heap of mirth, the tears streaming down her face.

There was something 'not quite the ticket' affecting the eldest daughter who was never called upon to do anything which required intelligence, but it did not prevent her from becoming a contralto in the chorus at the Old Vic.

She also gave piano and singing lessons, but the pupils must have found their surroundings and their teacher a matter of constant surprise.

The middle daughter (a violinist) was the most businesslike member of the family. I got the impression that she felt some embarrassment when dealing with her pupils, as there were so many hazards to overcome before they reached the room where all the lessons took place. Even then several nesting cats had to be removed.

The younger daughter played the cello and the three formed a trio which performed locally. How they ever reached their engagements on time is a mystery!

Whereas our clinically-reared family succumbed to all the childish illnesses, including the dreaded diphtheria, my cousins came through unscathed, obviously having built up an immune state both of mind and body which protected them.

Having them as relations was undoubtedly a bonus, and an experience which my children and grandchildren have not had the opportunity to enjoy.

- Biddy Rutson

One of the sons had been sentenced to ten years transportation to Tasmania for sheep-stealing in Suffolk... Matthew had been sentenced to be hung for stealing pigs in Norfolk...

I HAVE long since wanted to know about my grandpa and still do. He was born in Suffolk nearly 150 years ago, and it is to him, I believe, that I owe a long career in Fleet Street and my enthusiasm for gardening - although I never knew him.

Family history is now one of the fastest-growing hobbies in the country. Hundreds of thousands are involved in it.

The search for grandpa and my family has been long.

One lunch hour in London I went to the General Register Office at St Catherine's House, Kingsway. From a memorial card dated 1911 I knew that grandpa William Jerman, was 64 when he died. So he was born in 1847. I pulled down a heavy index volume from the shelves.

I found that a James Jerman, born in the workhouse at Bury St Edmunds, had been the son of Eliza German (sic), an illiterate pauper. No father was named. But I knew my grandpa was a William and not a James.

I began searching for his children. He married three times, so I had step-aunts and uncles.

There were ten in all and one by one I found them. I found that my step-aunt Agnes Eliza (was that name significant I wondered?) had been born in Plaistow, East London, in 1880.

I went to a local library which holds the 1881 Census. Yes, I found my grandpa. And the census said he had been born at Thorpe, Suffolk. Today there is no such place. It used to be Thorpe-by-Ixworth, but is now known as Ixworth Thorpe. So I wrote to the minister.

One Sunday evening there was an exciting phone call.

The minister confirmed that his church registers were still at the church.

"I have taken the liberty (*liberty!*) of looking through them," he said, "and I think I have found what you are looking for. We baptised a James William Jerman, son of Eliza German, in November, 1847. And in 1852 we married her and William Simper, a shepherd".

I had found my grandpa and his mother! I sent the minister a bottle of wine.

I realised later why he had dropped the James (though he named one of his sons that). It was customary for the eldest son to be named after his father, so to hide the illegitimacy the James had been dropped because the step-father was a William Simper.

I did not realise what I had begun.

William Jerman with the author's father on his knee. With them is a daughter by a previous marriage

Eliza was widowed early. She herself died at the great age of 88 and was buried at Ixworth Thorpe in 1911 - the same year my grandpa had died in London. I have seen the pretty churchyard in which she is buried. There is no stone. She was poor all her life and worked as a domestic servant.

From the 1861 Census I found that grandpa was still living in the village, aged 14. But by the 1871 Census he had vanished.

I was fortunate. Before starting my search I had talked with older relatives. They were even able to give me Jerman's three marriage certificates.

He first married Hannah Hammond at St George the Martyr, Southwark, London in 1868. He was a carman at Borough Market near London Bridge. I do not know what happened to him between the ages of 14 and 21.

He moved often in search of work. He became a gardener and lived at Penge and Carshalton.

Cordelia Jerman, who, with her husband, started a newsagents business

Hannah, alas, died young of tuberculosis, a scourge in cities at that time. Some of the children also died.

It was then I confirmed a piece of family oral history - that while living in Sydenham he was gardener to John Scott Russell, the engineer who built Isambard Kingdom Brunel's "Great Eastern" liner at Millwall.

By chance I was able to obtain from Lewisham Borough Library a map of the very garden he worked on! While there he showed grapes at the Crystal Palace which he had grown under glass. The greenhouses are on the map.

Jerman next married Emma Curtis at West Ham. There were several more children some of whom I have known well. But, sadly, she too soon died, also of consumption.

In 1890 grandpa married my grandmother, Cordelia. They had more children, the eldest my father. They started a paper business. In an old directory I found "W. and C. Jerman and Son, Newsagents." The son was my father, aged only eight!

I began wanting to know more about Eliza, my great grandma. I wrote to a Suffolk paper in search of a picture. None came.

But four months later an airmail letter dropped on the mat. It was from Queensland, Australia. Mrs. Sandra McNeill, who had written it, also sent me her family tree.

She told me we are sixth cousins! At the top of her tree are the same couple as at mine. Her maiden name was Middleditch. My paternal great-great-grandmother's name had been Middleditch. Someone had sent my letter out to Sandra.

Eliza German's mother, Ann Middleditch, had had three illegitimate sons, John, James and William, before marrying my great-great-grandpa, Robert German (sic) in 1810 in Suffolk. Now I knew why Eliza, my great-grandma, had named her son in the workhouse James William - after her elder step-brothers!

One of the sons, James, said Sandra, had been sentenced to ten years transportation to Tasmania for sheep stealing in Suffolk. But more, Ann Middleditch's brother Matthew had been sentenced to be hung for stealing pigs at Blo' Norton, Norfolk. But he was reprieved and also sent to Tasmania. He was Sandra's great-great-grandpa.

I now know I have many blood relatives in Tasmania, Australia and New Zealand. And I know a lot about many of them.

The search goes on, I know a little about Robert German, my great-great-grandfather. He lived at Stanton, Suffolk, and was born in the late 1700s. His parents were Edward German (or Jermin) and Elizabeth (nee Bass). They came from the Botesdale/Redgrave area of Suffolk.

My father inherited grandpa Jerman's paper business.

Thus I was able to read a lot, free of charge. My reading, and English, took me into Fleet Street and I went on to work as a journalist in twenty-five countries. I also watched my father in the garden. I have inherited his interests.

Looking for ones forebears is addictive. Every weekday up to 4,000 people descend on the General Register Office in London. They have their own magazine, and many are members of county history societies. They have some of the same excitements as I do.

In my spare time I am a prison visitor and am now retired. One day I was waiting to see an inmate at a Portsmouth jail. I chatted with an old nutbrown woman. She said: "This is fascinating. It sounds just like a book. Do you feel you know all these people now?"

I said: "Yes I do. At night when I close my bedroom door, they are all with me" - as they are, since I have their genes.

I said I thought the question was very perceptive, and how had it occurred to her. She replied: "Oh, I am a gypsy!" as though that explained it all.

- Leslie Jerman

WELL IT'S A JOB...

***When I announced I was going to be
a goblin, my Aunt Maggie said,
to an assenting chorus of disapproval:
"You're not going to wear that, Jeannie!"***

EVELYN R. MATHIAS

STRICTLY speaking, my first job was not really work at all; at least not the sort of work I had been led to expect during my last school term when the staff were doing their best to prepare us for the wider world outside.

But having completed my education, I was marking time until my job in the Glasgow Library materialised. In the meantime I scanned the 'situations vacant' column of the Citizen.

There were not a lot in the hard times of the middle 30s, so I was delighted to find an advert asking for 'young girls, slim and under 5 feet in height'.

I fitted the bill so I applied for what turned out to be a request for 'goblins' for that well-known manufacturer of vacuum cleaners.

Back home my mother and aunts muttered dire warnings of young girls being lured away, and the dreadful fate that could await them; but when the appointment for an interview came they were somewhat mollified by the respectable tone of the letter, and the place of meeting.

This turned out to be a large chilly church hall filled that afternoon to capacity by what seemed like dozens of ex-schoolgirls, all small, all thin and all hopeful!

A stout impressive Highland woman interviewed us, discarding the impossibles and keeping the rest of us on a short-list at one side of the hall. Her martyred expression became more so as the afternoon wore on, until at last I found to my surprise that I was one of the chosen six (certainly not for intellectual ability, more to fit the costumes provided).

These were supplied on the spot and we were allowed to take them home in order to make any minor adjustments necessary. "But on no account," said the large lady firmly, "cut into the material!"

To say that my mother was less than pleased when she viewed this costume must be the understatement of that year.

It consisted of a red linen tunic with long sleeves and red tights which were then the perogative of pantomime Prince Charmings, ballet dancers and others who in my mother's eyes followed less-than-respectable professions.

The costume was completed with red leather shoes, slightly turned up at the toes as befits a goblin, and a close-fitting cap with large pointy ears.

"You're never going to wear *that* in public, Jeannie" said my

EVELYN R. MATHIAS

Aunt Maggie to a sort of Greek chorus of assenting disapproval in the background (from my mother and Aunt Nellie).

Surprisingly, my father, a cabinet-maker, did not disapprove. Perhaps he wanted his young daughter to have this 'fun' job before settling down to the serious business of earning a living.

He did, however, insist on meeting me each evening to bring me home; no easy task this as at that time, after the launching of the

Queen Mary he and his fellow artisans on the Clyde had moved in to complete the stateroom panelling and he was working very hard.

The Glasgow Trades Fair was that year held in the Kelvin Hall.

This was a pleasant environment and the work for the goblins was not too difficult - just handing out leaflets and passing any interested customers to the salesmen.

Only one goblin was required to be on duty at any one time on each of the three stalls, and in our spare time we toured the hall as walking advertisements. It was fascinating to see the latest styles in clothes shown by the fashion houses, the china, cutlery and so much more.

I can best recall the lovely meals in the restaurant where three small giggling goblins created something of a sensation.

To me, used as I was to the 'nourishing but plain' meals at home, this was something of a gourmet's paradise. We experimented wildly with Indian, Italian and Chinese dishes.

But all things come to an end. Soon it was time to wash, press and return my goblin's costume and to start my work in the library. Less fun, more poorly paid, but ultimately more rewarding.

As a very junior assistant my job was mainly to ensure that the books were kept in strict alphabetical order of authors.

However, all was not entirely routine. That was the year in which Margaret Mitchell's book Gone With the Wind was published, taking the Glasgow populace by storm.

Everyone, it seemed, wanted to read it, from the ladies of uncertain age who usually confined their reading to romantic fiction ("hiv you onything new in love stories, hen?") to hardbitten shipyard riveters fascinated by the American Civil War and impressed by the fact that this book had taken all of ten years to research by its authoress.

We had an unprecedented number of copies on loan, and whenever there was one available I borrowed it and read it bit by bit, sometimes over my lunch and tea breaks, but more often perched high on the library steps, oblivious that readers were choosing books below as I eagerly followed the fortunes of Scarlett, Rhett Butler and the rest.

- Jeannie Peck

*Like father, like son, Joe Taylor proud
proprietor, outside Central Stores in the 1930s*

What treasures there were - nutmegs, Turkey Rhubarb, ginger, Gregory powders and herbs. Boiling water was poured over sticks of liquorice and was kept in a bottle tucked away in a corner of the Yorkshire Range for whenever bowels needed a bit of assistance...

GRANDAD became a village grocer through a stroke of bad luck. John Taylor - born in 1865 - was an honest, upright, and trustworthy young man. But times were hard and, through no fault of his own, John, a young husband with a baby to rear, was sacked by his boss.

He took leave of the grocery establishment where he had been apprenticed one Saturday tea-time.

First thing Monday morning saw him taking the first steps to become a Grocer and Provision Merchant in his own right.

There wasn't much furniture in the small, stone cottage in the West Riding of Yorkshire. But John pulled the trestle table into the front window overlooking the road. On it he displayed his first commodity - half a pound of best butter.

A sign, in his best copper-plate handwriting, stated that he intended to become a grocer. He would deem it a favour if people of the village would patronise him, once established.

Hazel's grandfather, John Taylor, who took the first steps as Grocer and Provision Merchant

Wearing his best 'pepper and salt' suit, with a wicker basket over his arm, he strode the two miles into the town.

He called at the wholesaler, Cooper and Webb. He was known there and they allowed him credit on his first lot of grocery items.

Light of heart, the young man walked to the 'posh' end of town and knocked on house doors.

"Good morning, Madam. May I count on your valuable support to patronize John Taylor for your future grocery orders? I guarantee personal attention, prompt deliveries and the very best groceries available."

He soon had a list of prospective customers. John never owned a car, but the two iron 'sack carts' would serve admirably for delivering orders.

Next morning his wife Jane was left in charge of the make-do shop while John set off to deliver his first orders.

A great asset to the success of the new business was the jam-

56

Jane Taylor - she was left in charge as John delivered his first orders

making side. In fields nearby John's brother William had a market garden where he grew soft fruits and acres of rhubarb.

In the tiny scullery at the back Jane made delicious jams of umpteen varieties, as well as marmalade.

Out of the first small profits they bought a pair of brass weighing scales.

When John was absolutely sure that borrowing money for building a proper shop and attached house was a feasible proposition, he decided on a plot of land opposite their little low cottage.

Everything was to be of the best. Foundations were dug deep and the proud couple watched every step of the construction of 'Central Stores'.

When the outer structure, with its two large display windows, was completed, the excitement of choosing interior furnishings began.

From floor to ceiling in the living room/kitchen behind the shop they had large open shelves with deep drawers underneath for drapery. This was always referred to as 'The Fittings'.

The shelves were for trays of bread and teacakes, Yorkshire spice cake and other delicacies.

Drapery consisted mainly of men's striped working shirts, bloomers, stockings and combinations - those abominations with a slit at the front.

Packets of Mene sanitary towels were hidden away at the top of the fittings, never mentioned outright by name but always written down on a slip of paper handed to grandma.

Waist-high aluminium bins were fitted along one side of the shop for flour. Another was for sugar, one for hen corn - it was wonderful

A picture from the early days of Central Stores. Alf "the yeast man" is coming u

to run your fingers through that smooth, honey-gold Indian corn or make patterns in the flour with the big oval-shaped scoops.

A solid mahogany counter proudly awaited its first customers and behind it, fixed to the wall, neat rows of tiny drawers labelled with the name of their contents with gilt-edged labels.

What treasures there were - whole nutmegs, Turkey Rhubarb, ginger, Gregory powders and lots of herbs such as camomile, mint, hyssop, liquorice powder and Beechams Powders.

Shelves reached the ceiling housing all manner of items such as bottles of Indian Brandy, castor oil, jars of Vaseline, Zambuk and

e road. Hazel remembers playing "Puss, puss come to my corner" under the gaslamp

sticks of hard, jet-black liquorice wrapped in yellow leaves. Boiling water was poured over a stick of liquorice and was kept in a bottle tucked away in the corner of the Yorkshire Range. It was ready for a sup whenever bowels needed a bit of assistance.

On the cigarette shelf, twist, brown, flecked, and aromatic all lay coiled into flat, snake-like contortions in a tin box. A special sharp knife nipped off required ounces.

Open shelves beneath the counter housed packets of Acdo and Rinso washing powders, Colman's Starch, Dolly Blue, donkey stones for scouring doorsteps - a regular purchase on Friday mornings when housewives were preparing for the weekend.

Then there were tins of Brasso and Silvo, the soft newness of yellow dusters, skipping ropes, whips and tops, packets of chalk, marbles, shuttlecocks and battledores.

From the ceiling lethal iron hooks held rolls of home-cured ham and bacon. Huge round marble containers in a recess housed butter, lard and cheese. The wooden boxes in which cheeses were delivered were pounced upon with glee for covering the young shoots of rhubarb in the back garden.

John Taylor established himself in a business that was to flourish through two world wars - all from one half pound of butter.

- Hazel Wheeler

Hazel aged 10

The one thing I shall always remember about my first job is that wonderful smell of freshly-baked bread...

SOON after leaving school at 14 I started work at a small family bakery in Walmer, near Deal in Kent. I started work at 6.30am in the bakehouse so people would have their hot rolls for breakfast. At 7.30 I started off on my round.

I had a large basket with the rolls carefully wrapped in a clean white cloth to keep them warm. I would start off along Downs Road ringing a small hand bell on a leather strap. Quite often I would sell out before going the whole round.

On Good Friday morning we used to deliver hot cross buns in time for breakfast. Preparing of the dough would start on Thursday evening and baking went on through the night.

I would start early on Good Friday morning packing up the various orders that I had taken the previous week into bags and loading them into the large 'tallboy' basket that fitted onto the carrier cycle. Then off I would go as fast as I could.

For Easter we made currant buns, butter buns and spice buns. They cost one old penny each and were twice the size of the ones you buy today.

For my morning round I had a large, high, specially built two-wheeled bakers' barrow. It held quite a lot of bread and was heavy when full.

At the back were two iron rods with a tiny iron wheel to prevent it from tipping backwards. At the front were two wooden flaps to protect the inside and a drawer at the bottom for bags of self-raising flour and cakes.

At the start of the round, when the barrow was full and rather heavy, to stop it I leaned back on the handles and slid on my boots till it came to a halt!

I did the small afternoon delivery on a carrier cycle with the large 'tallboy' basket on the front full of bread.

-Walter Janaway

Occasionally, I was sent with a message into the main works, and would linger briefly admiring the speed of the women decorating and packing the chocolates...

THE recession of the twenties and thirties hit almost every family and my father was affected like everyone else; my mother took in lodgers to help with the housekeeping.

Money was very short and young people leaving school had to take any job they could get and be grateful.

We lived on the outskirts of Birmingham and someone told me that Cadbury Brothers of Bournville would be taking on staff in September to prepare for the extra Christmas trade.

So I decided to apply to the firm, enclosing the necessary references supplied by my headmaster and the local vicar. I was

Decorating chocolates in the Cadbury factory... a skilled job done at speed

accepted on a temporary basis.

Until I arrived that first morning I had no idea what my work would consist of, but it was a start, a means of earning money to help my parents. I remember that with my first week's pay, I put a deposit on our first wireless set and paid off the rest week by week. I felt quite important.

The job, in the gift department, was messy and monotonous, but was lightened by the cheery camaraderie amongst the other girls.

In those days cocoa, you will remember, was a cheap and nourishing drink, and small coupons like stamps were put into the packets.

Customers saved them and stuck them into books. Then they were able to choose gifts from a catalogue, varying the items in value according to the number saved.

This was very popular among housewives as a means of obtaining a few extras for home and children. Thousands of letters arrived at the factory every day, increasing greatly in the weeks leading up to Christmas.

We had to count these coupons and check that the right amount had been sent for the required articles. We were provided with overalls and caps, and also finger stalls to protect our nails. On opening the envelopes we found many coupons were smothered in cocoa powder; some had got wet and were stuck together in a gooey mess.

The Cadbury family was very forward-looking and there were many facilities, including a swimming bath, in the grounds. We were also encouraged to continue our studies and were allowed day release to attend college, hopefully to improve our status.

Prizes were given for suggestions to increase the profits and improve working conditions, and everyone had the chance to buy shares in the company.

Occasionally, I was sent with a message into the main works, and would linger briefly admiring the speed of the women decorating and packing the chocolates, then go on into the cocoa department where the tins were made, filled and labelled.

During my time at Cadburys, preparations were going on everywhere for the coronation of Edward VIII, and our firm was as busy as others producing special creations for the great day.

We young girls did not know much about the rumours that were

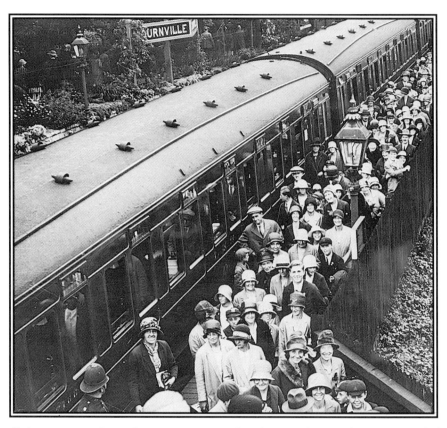

flying around, so it was a great shock one day to hear a special announcement, during the lunchtime music programme, telling us of the abdication.

This must have caused quite a loss to the company, as all the new designs and packaging had to be scrapped. I still have one of the chocolate boxes made for the occasion, with the King's head on the lid.

After the Christmas rush I was taken on permanently and given a much nicer position in one of the offices.

- Pat Williamson

The kitchen was my domain, or so I thought... Then Cook led me to a scullery where I would be spending a lot of time washing up and preparing all the vegetables...

I WAS 14 when I went 'into place' in a large house in the country as a kitchenmaid - yet what I knew about kitchens was nothing , and what I wanted to know was even less.

Even though many of us were not in the least domesticated, it was the accepted thing to do.

I arrived in the country by bus. After living in a town the silence was deafening as I walked through rolling parkland to The Hall.

The front door was open and I could see a large entrance hall leading to a wide, thick-carpeted staircase - the likes of which I had only seen before in films.

How was I to know that only the chauffeured guests came in this way and everyone else used the back door?

The housemaid who answered the bell hustled me quickly through the plush rooms and up the back stairs to the attic bedroom with a sloping roof that we were to share. When I looked out of the window it was like being in the middle of nowhere with a lot of sheep.

But the kitchen was my domain, or so I thought. It was huge and so was everything in it.

A large Aga cooker stood against one wall, large copper pans on shelves against another, there was a Welsh dresser and a large well-scrubbed table in the middle.

Cook said I would not be spending too much time in here, and led me into the next large room which was the scullery where, apparently, I would spend a great deal of time doing all the washing up and preparing all the vegetables after I had collected them from the gardener.

A black contraption in the corner was a stove that had to be raked out and lit every morning, banked up with coke and blackleaded every day.

Learning the rules of life in service.
These girls were attending a school for maids

The next large adjoining room was the pantry that seemed carved out of stone with stone slabs around the walls and a stone floor.

Large bowls filled to the brim with milk stood on these slabs with thick cream settled on top. I could hardly wait to start creaming it off.

The best was yet to come.

The servants' hall was another large, but cosy, room with a long table set for tea with white bread and brown, ham and tongue, chutney and jam, fruit and cream. Better than tea at home!

The other servants were already in place and the arrival of Cook was the signal to start eating.

Good food, lively company, a view of pasture from the window - what a 'place' downstairs!

The months that followed were full to overflowing - up early to light the stove, help prepare breakfast, wash the pots and pans, scrub the tables, floors and steps.

Then it was time to collect the fruit and vegetables. It was time to visit the Garden of Eden.

To step through the door of the large walled garden was to step into another world. Everything grew here - vegetables, flowers, herbs and fruit trees. In the greenhouse peaches, grapes, tomatoes and cucumbers flourished.

After sharing the gardener's cheese sandwiches for elevenses, we would tour the garden, selecting what would be needed for the Hall that day. I would return to the house with laden baskets but not before sampling the luscious fruits.

Most afternoons we were free to do what we wanted and we roamed the countryside, cycled to the village, or visited the farm next door. Then it was back to the grindstone in the evening to prepare dinner for 'them upstairs' and sometimes for large dinner parties.

It was a long day, but the abundance of food gave us energy.

We relaxed at the end of the day in the servants' hall where we played cards, talked, wrote letters or listened to the wireless. Sometimes we went to a whist drive in the village and occasionally to a dance that went on until two o'clock in the morning.

My first ever dance was a momentous occasion. We had bought lengths of material from a travelling salesman and the parlourmaid made us long dance dresses on a treadle sewing machine.

We bought silver dance shoes from the village shop on weekly instalments and, suitably attired, we were chauffeured to the dance.

Who cared if we couldn't dance a step - being dressed up was enough.

War brought the changes. Those who were old enough left to join the Forces or to do war work. Dinner parties ceased and we who were left knitted balaclavas, scarves and gloves for the troops.

When it was time for me to go I left with fond memories of being 'in place' - downstairs.

Unfortunately I did not learn to be domesticated or to be a good cook. But I did learn how to dance, play whist, milk a cow, ride a horse, to enjoy gardening and have a deep appreciation of country life.

- Olga King

She taught us how to cover the heads with chalk so that they spun with the colours of the rainbow...

OUR Nanny didn't have any letters after her name or any special qualifications except a recommendation from her brother Fred who served in the Royal Marines.

When based at Plymouth, Fred was a regular customer at the Harvest Home Hotel of which my father was proprietor.

Knowing that my mother was expecting her third child, it was Fred who persuaded her to see his sister Doris who was mad about children and would make a good nursemaid.

So it was that Doris Ellerby came to us straight from school at the age of fifteen.

At that time I was almost three, my sister Barbara was toddling and the third baby was expected quite soon.

My earliest recollection of Doris - who became known by us all as Nanny - was to make the discovery of her shoes and stockings on a day when I had crept into her bedroom, unseen.

The thrill of pushing my small legs into grey lisle stockings, of standing in her pointed-toed shoes and being caught in the act, will always be remembered.

At the large public house there were eight bedrooms - Nanny's being the one next to me and my sister. Our two grandmothers who lived with us could never speak too highly of the young woman with the grey eyes who had such a way with children and who could put her hand to anything asked of her.

Quite soon Nanny was taken by my mother to be measured for a traditional nursemaid's uniform which included the wearing of a white bib apron, stiff white collar and cuffs, a floating veil held in place by a tight band across the forehead and a wide white belt around the waist.

By the time I was six, I could knit. Nanny's steel knitting needles were forever creating jerseys, dresses, and Fair Isle jumpers for us. She was a natural pianist and she'd wash the car as happily as she'd wash our Cocker spaniel.

When business was hectic in the public or saloon bars, she didn't

Doris the Nanny - pianist, knitter and ever-willing helper who would wash a car or a Cocker spaniel

need to be asked a second time whether she'd mind giving a hand.

She helped us with everything. Puzzles, painting competitions, how to spin tops and to cover the heads with chalk so that when they were spinning fast they'd spin all the colours of the rainbow. She taught us to play Snap and Strip Jack Naked, how to do French crotchet, and the words of popular songs.

She made many conquests. I was ten when she left us to get married and to live in London where her own three children were born.

Apart from birthday and Christmas cards, we hadn't seen Doris Ellerby in fifty years - until 1984 when she decided she must see the children she had nursed during the twenties. We looked forward with delight to seeing her again. When she stepped from the coach in Liverpool as smartly dressed and erect as ever for her seventy-nine years, it was obvious she had changed but little.

She fell in love with Liverpool and enjoyed the Garden Festival of that year. Having spent a week with me, she made the journey to Plymouth where my sister and brother revived old memories by taking her for a walk across Plymouth Ho! where in those long ago days she had pushed each of us in our prams.

Doris Ellerby died at the age of 87 in June 1992 having lived a healthy energetic life without illness.

She never stopped knitting or playing the piano. She was a bingo fanatic and MC at her local old people's club in Hampshire. I have only to walk through the parks and places of my childhood to be reminded of our wonderful Nanny.

- Nina Kenworthy

ALL PART OF THE SERVICE

I once had to remove a small finger from a medicine bottle. Mum had tried by wrapping the bottle in a towel and attacking it with a hammer...

I SPENT ten happy years working in a chemist shop in a small village. I knew all the local folk and their complaints, and I was kept well-informed on all the latest scandal. Each day brought a different set of people with prescriptions to dispense and while they waited you heard the case history, which was sometimes laughable, and often very sad.

My face must have suggested I was a good listener because so many customers poured out their troubles and secrets that I felt the least I could do was stand and listen.

The changing seasons brought different complaints.

The school children would all catch athlete's foot and require cream and powder. Then it was cough mixture time. At holiday times it was calamine lotions, and campers wanting water-purifying tablets and insect repellents.

Mums would rush in with screaming children who had grazed

knees, or had fallen out of the pram and needed instant treatment. Often it only required a sweet and a plaster to cure the trouble. A kind word from the chemist worked wonders.

I once had trouble removing a small finger from a medicine bottle, but a liberal helping of grease freed it. The child's mother had tried several methods, including wrapping the bottle and the hand in a towel and attacking it with a large hammer. It's small wonder the poor kid had screamed and gone stiff with fright!

One small boy was dragged in with a very distorted face. He had had a nose bleed and his dear mother had spent ten minutes and a packet of cotton wool, plugging his nostril. When the child saw himself in the mirror looking like a hamster with a mouthful of nuts, he was terrified.

He was soon dealt with and went off happy, sucking a free lolly.

Our pharmacist was very good at his job but rather on the eccentric side. He was keen cyclist, but after a full day's work he got rather tired (after all he *was* over sixty).

So he would cycle into the countryside, get off his bike for a rest and fall asleep.

Several folk thought he was dead when they found him asleep on the grass verge. One time he chained his cycle to a tree, lost the key and had to catch a bus home, to return the next day with a hacksaw and cut through the chain.

On another day, in spring, he decided to prune the apple tree which grew behind the shop. After about three hours we went to find him and found he was stuck up the tree - it needed the firemen and their ladder to bring him down.

With all his peculiar little ways everyone liked him. I never had one cross word with him, and only moved on because he decided to retire when decimal coinage was introduced.

As a boss I'll give him top marks.

- Kay Martin

I found the Americans very friendly.
Two of them dug my garden for me
and I found oranges and sweets left
in the kitchen. They needed something
to mark the end of their convoy
and left with my green petticoat
fluttering in the breeze...

WHEN I was eleven I decided I wanted to have a home-made cake shop and cafe when I was grown up. My dream came true when a friend of my mother's and myself became partners and found a shop in a Worcestershire village. We started our venture at the cafe two days after war broke out. I remember saying, "Thank goodness the business is dealing in food" (as we also sold tinned goods and sweets). "Even if there is a war, people have to eat!"

We were on a main road with parking space in front, and near a bus stop. The station was three minutes walk away, so it was in a good position.

I made the cakes and my partner served the customers. The first week or two were rather hectic as a school from Felixstowe had been evacuated to the village and the teachers used to come in for their tea.

Unfortunately the previous owner had gradually let the business go down and there was only £20 worth of stock when we took over. We realised things would be difficult to obtain so decided to pay ourselves only 5/- per week and put the rest of the profit into stock.

Later we were glad of this as, when rationing started, we were based on a proportion of the previous year's output. As it cost me 2/6 to go home each weekend, I had only 2/6 to exist on though, of course, we had our food out of the business.

I remember on my half day I used to walk three miles to the nearest town, take sandwiches and sit in the 6d seats at the cinema for rest and amusement. If I was lucky, I had the fare to take the bus home, otherwise I walked.

After a few months, most of the Felixstowe children and teachers returned home. We then had a lot of Welsh soldiers for several months, which made us busy again.

They came for special training before being sent abroad.

In 1941 my partner's husband persuaded her to give up her share of the business.

I decided I would try and manage on my own, borrowing £100 from my father to buy her share. Unfortunately all the furniture except that in my bedroom belonged to her, so I had to furnish two sitting rooms and a bedroom.

I applied for furniture coupons but the application was turned down, so I went to auctions and bought some from customers. I was able to let a bedroom and sitting room to two lady teachers.

Rationing made things difficult and I remember one awful day I discovered the tin with my sweet coupons in had been thrown in the dustbin by mistake; fortunately I was able to retrieve them before the bin was emptied.

One of the silly restrictions was that you could put sugar in the cakes, but if the top had sugar sprinkled on, you were liable to a fine.

One day we heard that an American Army Medical Corps (women and men) were to be billeted in the village. As you can imagine, this caused great excitement as they had to be put in private houses. They would have their meals in a large central hut built specially for the purpose.

This made me very busy again. Their favourite was strong coffee with hot sausage rolls plastered with French mustard. They asked me if I could remain open in the evenings for those who didn't want to go to the pub, but I hadn't the rations or staff to enable me to do this.

I must say I found the Americans friendly and helpful; two of them dug my garden for me and several times I found oranges and sweets left in the kitchen. My friends and I took it in turns to invite several of the female nurses to our homes in the evening so got to know them quite well.

After several months they were sent abroad but before they went they asked me if I had anything green I could let them have to put on the back of the last truck of the convoy to show it was the end.

Though it was a lighter green than intended, I found a green

74

petticoat, so the convoy set off with my petticoat fluttering in the breeze!

After they left I found ten pounds of sugar left in the kitchen, which was a great help.

Life had to go on. There were several weddings in the village and I was asked to make the wedding cakes. As rations were so scarce, I had to ask them for sugar and margarine to help out. One lady brought butter saying, "I have given my husband margarine instead of butter and he didn't know the difference!"

Making these cakes was a great responsibility as the ingredients couldn't be replaced, but I am glad to say they all turned out well.

Each weekend when I went home I took part of my ration of meat, butter, sugar and tea as I couldn't expect my family to give me theirs. One of my customers occasionally let me have a few new laid eggs, which was a great help. The cakes had to be made with dried eggs, but sometimes I was allowed a large tin of frozen eggs which made better cakes.

Several times a year the local clergyman had a service, then a working breakfast in the rectory. They asked me if I could provide breakfast for about twelve.

I gave them fish cakes, tea, toast, marmalade and butter. I remember what a lot of fun and laughter there was during the meal and how I enjoyed serving them.

Some of us were asked to help the local farmers and the first job we had to do was to 'single' beet. This was hard on the back as the rows were very long and the first time it was difficult to straighten my back after bending for so long. We got paid for this but we all agreed to give the money to charity.

One evening I had been visiting friends several miles away and, while waiting for a bus, I noticed a red glow in the sky in the far distance. I discovered afterwards that it was the flames from the terrible air raid on Coventry.

Memories come flooding back.

I remember the morning the 'phone rang and, on answering it, I was told it was the police. Fortunately all they wanted was a large pot of tea for twenty-two policemen who were playing a football match at the back and wanted cups of tea at half-time as lemons were still difficult to obtain.

After this I often made tea for them, so got on the right side of the law!

As the months went by, rations became easier and I was able to cater for cricket teas in the summer and hockey teas in the winter. I had to use my downstairs sitting room or garden for this in order to leave the small cafe free for casual customers.

One Saturday the local hunt met outside my cafe which lent a splash of colour to the scene. (I also got some fertiliser for my garden!)

After 17 years of a busy but interesting time, due to family reasons, I had to sell my business and return home.

I still go back to visit my friends, but find the village much changed with many more houses and shops. The last time I saw my shop and cafe it was empty and looked neglected, which made me feel sad.

I have since heard that it is now a good restaurant, which I hope to visit next time I go back to the village.

- May Roberts

IN THE late 1920s the 'Perm' had just come to our small town and only one hairdresser had permanent wave equipment installed.

She had only a few rollers, so half the head was done at a time. Then the rollers were fastened to a sort of metal wheel, rather like a small bicycle wheel, and the whole thing was suspended from the ceiling.

A lady having her hair done would find that her scalp grew hotter and hotter, and steam rose to the ceiling; not even a cup of tea helped to ease the discomfort.

After a cooling-off period, the hair was released from the rollers and there they lay - real curls!

In fact, they were somewhat corkscrewy and rather like little brown caterpillars. One just couldn't wait until the other side was 'done', washed and set.

This took up a whole day with a short interval for a packed lunch and cost somewhere from £6 to £12.

But it was worth it, though one had to have a 'set' at intervals to make the whole thing last about six months.

- Eva Churchman

PUTTING ON THE STYLE

We called at the shop and bought rock, had a look at the saucy postcards, and it was all aboard again...

I WILL never forget the happy days we used to spend with our own charabanc. We had saved a shilling a week for the year and now the day had arrived at last.

It was a lovely sunny morning when we began to arrive at the little local pub yard and there she stood, our 'Joybelle', paint gleaming, big brass lamps, horn with rubber 'honker', steering column polished to look like gold. Standing beside her was the driver complete with dust coat and peaked hat with goggles on "in case of dusty roads".

Her hood was down as it looked as if the sun would shine all day.

The landlord of the pub was packing the refreshments in the back, one bottle of beer for going, another for coming home, with lemonade for those who preferred it.

We all climbed aboard, waved our goodbyes to the little knot of folk who had come to see us off, and were away, heading for Felixstowe on the Suffolk coast.

We hadn't got very far when someone said they were thirsty, so the driver pulled into a side lane and we had our bottle. Some people were still thirsty, so they had the one for coming home.

Then it was 'spend a penny' time - free that day as we were miles from anywhere.

I still smile about it, ladies one side of the road behind the hedge, gentlemen to the other side.

I can still see a row of heads a few feet apart, looking down like they were having a two-minute silence. We ladies kept well down in case of 'Peeping Toms'. Then it was all aboard once again, and we were off.

We arrived at Felixstowe at midday and were told to meet later at the restaurant where our lunch had been arranged. We went our separate ways, ladies making for the shops and some of the gents making for the nearest pub (after all, it was the "pub outing", they said).

We made our way to the restaurant and were shown to a large room set aside especially for parties. We took our seats and were handed a menu. There were several roast meats and vegetables, but for some reason fish and chips at the seaside always smell and taste so much better than they do at home so most of us had them with apple pie or ice creams and coffee afterwards.

We came out into the sunshine once more, and again split up. Some sat in the lovely gardens, some played a round of clock golf, others - me included - took deck chairs down to the water's edge to see the children play. We watched the boats leaving from Harwich Quay to the Hook of Holland, and wondered what they were carrying.

We had a snooze, only to be woken either by a dog that had been in the water, shaking itself over us, or the deck chair man collecting his money.

Someone mentioned having a cup of tea so we made our way to a little beach cafe where they were serving shrimp teas (if you've

All set for a chara outing.
This lot don't look as happy as the people who rode in Joybelle!

never had a Harwich shrimp tea, I'm afraid you have missed one of life's little luxuries).

Our time was running out and we had to be back at the charabanc, so we called at the shop and bought rock for the children and friends, and had a quick look at the saucy postcards, then it was all aboard once again.

We called at a small inn kept by a friend of our local publican - he had been told we would be calling - and sat at little tables on the green. He had provided lovely crusty bread rolls and cheese and big jars of pickled onions, eggs and gherkins.

It was getting dusk when we arrived home. Our landlord and landlady were there to meet us, and we all went into the club-room where tables were set.

They brought in great dishes of lovely brown, sizzling sausages and great heaps of mash, washed down with whatever we fancied.

When we had finished, we talked about what we had done, and showed each other the things we had bought or won.

One chap had a pocket watch he had won at hoopla. It had cost him a fortune and stopped as soon as Joybelle had and was 'never to go again'.

We all went home, and if we were up half the night with indigestion and felt a bit fragile the next day, it was well worth it.

Soon they were getting a list of names together and we started saving our shillings, ready for the next outing with our dear old Joybelle.

- M. Herbert

In our first Way You Were booklet, Gordon Marriott described his love affair with a Velocette motorbike called 'Alice'. Now comes a story of passion about Dot from Wolverhampton...

TO THOSE who may think this is yet another tale of sexual conquest I must say you'll be disappointed. However, to those who remember motorcycling before the Japanese 'revolution', when the machines had real character, then read on.

Dot arrived in 1956, taking her name from the makers DOT motorcycles of Wolverhampton, who were more famous for their successful competition bikes than for road machines.

As a consequence she was endowed with the characteristics of both types but, as is normal with hybrids, was not strong in either, causing her to develop a powerful personality of her own.

Dot was built more for convenience than show - no gleaming make-up for her. Her frame was painted matt grey and a single coat of blue varnish covered the petrol tank, her only adornment being chrome on her handlebars and headlamp rim.

In addition, she had no rear suspension which made long journeys somewhat uncomfortable but this was offset by 'state of the art' telescopic front forks which, although admirable as shock absorbers, were prone to high-pitch squeaking if not given a dose of oil on a very regular basis.

Dot's heart was a two-stroke engine which, when all was well, never missed a beat.

However, if conditions were not exactly to her liking, she would complain in no uncertain terms by either whiskering the plug, allowing the carburettor to flood, or just defiantly refusing to start.

When she was really angry she allowed herself to get so overheated that it brought about a temporary seizure, leaving me to wait until she decided to cool off enough to allow our journey to continue.

It wasn't long before I discovered Dot had a rather sadistic sense of humour which showed itself in a variety of ways.

She developed the knack of vibrating loose the ignition lead which would then land on my right foot sending the voltage from the magneto through my leg.

One particularly nasty prank was to cause the carburettor float to stick which invariably filled my shoes with petrol.

Another little trick was to strip the teeth off the front drive sprocket which always happened when I was on my way to somewhere important like the pub or the cinema.

After incidents such as these the engine always seemed to make a noise akin to someone chuckling.

Another quirk was the unreliability of Dot's clutch mechanism which was a constant headache and on more than one occasion the clutchplate had to be repaired with wine bottle corks.

In fact I got very good at going into pubs and asking for a few discarded corks, ignoring the strange looks and such remarks as "Are you sure you wouldn't like some chewing gum and string as well?".

Like most ladies, Dot was jealous of other females in which I showed even a passing interest.

One pillion passenger got a nasty burn on her leg from the silencer when Dot unceremoniously unseated the pair of us after an attempt to climb a greasy knoll.

Under normal conditions the climb would not have been a problem but, with a lady passenger, no way!

On another occasion, when I foolishly allowed my future wife to drive, Dot jammed her throttle wide open and it was more by sheer providence than anything else that we managed to avoid disaster.

This tale would not be complete without reference to Dot's lighting system which, for most of the time, might as well have been non-existent.

The lights only worked if the engine was running at a reasonable rate so, at low speeds on a dark night, it was very difficult to see the road ahead, as the light given off resembled the output of the average glow-worm.

Dot was very unforgiving if she was not fed her favourite petrol and oil mixture, a fact that was brought sharply home to me when a new-fangled pump at my local garage failed to mix oil and petrol in the correct ratio and she rewarded me by seizing solid and pitching me over the handlebars into the nearest field.

Repairs were lovingly carried out on the kitchen table much to the annoyance of my mother who threatened, for the umpteenth time, to throw us both out into the street.

On starting National Service I handed Dot to my brother, thus ending a three-year love-hate relationship which, although fraught with difficulties, can never be forgotten not only for the pleasure it gave but also for the roadsense it taught, a sense which has proved more than useful throughout my many years as a road-user.

- Anthony Cokayne

Madam was on the small side and slim but she had the gyrating power of a wound-up gramophone spring...

IN MY youth, when the foxtrot and the quickstep were popular small dance halls proliferated. In Salford they were called 'jiggers' and there was one at the end of our street.

At that time my 16-year-old pal was mad keen to learn dancing but loath to go alone, so he nagged at me until I agreed to go with him to a dancing school he knew of.

The 'school', a couple of rooms over a shop, was run by a Madam Jones. The first half hour of the evening was a beginners class for boys. To take part cost sixpence.

I was hesitant. I had heard that the 'quality' knew the lower classes as 'the great unwashed', so on the night of our trial foray into the world of scent and sequins, I made myself as presentable as possible.

I had a stripped-off scrub in the slopstone. Like others of the period our slopstone was a brown, glazed pot and almost large enough to bathe in. As a finishing touch I plastered my hair down with solid brilliantine.

Ready for action, we set out for where Madam Jones catered for apprentice gigolos.

In our local picture house I'd watched the flickering image of Fred Astaire and envied his polished performance as he whirled a beautiful partner across a ballroom floor.

But now this same prospect lay before me I felt strangely reluctant to grasp the opportunity. In fact, the nearer we got the slower progress became. We eventually braved the staircase, paid our sixpences, and sat in chairs ranged round the room, awaiting our fate.

Madam Jones, resplendent in ankle-length dance frock, clapped her hands to gain attention, then, to piano accompaniment demonstrated various dance steps. She did this twice, then brought us to our feet en masse and talked us through the steps without the piano.

It was some sight!

A dozen or so lads - most of us with two left feet and no sense of

84

rhythm - lumbering round the room, each doing his own interpretation of Madam's shouted instructions.

At Madam's signal we resumed our seats.

"Gentlemen, your attention please. Before we dismiss I will give a short demonstration." She caught one of the lads by the hand.

"If you wouldn't mind?" she smiled sweetly.

The piano struck up a quickstep. Madam was on the small side and slim, but she had the gyrating power of a wound-up gramophone spring. She spun her partner round like a rag doll caught up in a tornado.

And she was clever. In those few hectic minutes the embarrassed lad kicked his ankles and trod on *his* feet but his shoes never touched her toes. She saw to that.

Going home my pal asked, "What d'you think Jack?"

I was cautious, "Not bad".

"Shall we go again?"

I replied, "Yes - but if she tries that caper on me I'll tell her to go and eat coke. She enjoyed making that chap look daft".

For the next three weeks at the close of the session Madam played the same trick on some unsuspecting newcomer.

The fourth week we were seated behind her and she turned to face us. Looking her straight in the eye I returned her smile with my well-practised George Raft sneer. So she grabbed my pal.

Two minutes later she cast him into his chair with the air of someone dropping something in a dustbin.

For as long as I'd known him my friend had had a barely noticeable nervous tic, his head twitched ever so slightly. Now he was red-faced, breathless and his head was twitching like crazy.

He followed her progress across the room with blazing eyes then, in a voice too low for anyone else to hear, he breathed, "You rotten devil."

On the way home he didn't speak.

The incident put the kybosh on our dancing lark. He never mithered me to go again.

- Jack Jackson

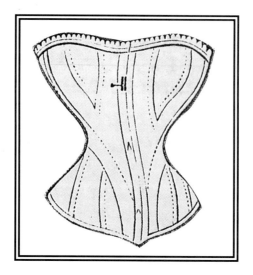

DURING the war, while hubby was away in the Army, they held dances each Friday night just across the road from where we lived. On one occasion I decided to go with two or three other soldiers' wives.

I had been brought up to wear lace-backed corsets so, I went off to the dance wearing them.

The bones were sticking into me so much I decided to go to the cloakroom and take the horrible things off. The only place to put them was up my coat sleeve. I went on with the dancing.

When it came to the last waltz I went with my friends to the cloakroom for my coat.

Imagine the colour of my face when I put one arm in my coat and the corsets fell to the floor.

- Mrs E Henry

SMOKE GETS IN YOUR EYES

My brother finished his roll-up and although my pipe was not yet empty, I knocked it out. "Gotta chew some grass now" he said, "so they can't smell the smoke on your breath..."

HAVE any of you out there tried to give up smoking? Of course you have! "But I just can't do it," you say. "I've tried lots of times, but I just can't. Besides I enjoy a smoke."

That's just what I said but I finally did give it up.

Oh, I tried many times over the years all to no avail. Magic expensive courses of tablets somehow made me increase my smoking instead of giving it up. After sucking on a dummy cigarette for ten minutes I would immediately light up a real one.

I smoked all brands of cigarettes including foreign, but for most of the time I rolled my own. There again I rolled almost every brand of tobacco on the market.

Mostly, though, I rolled up pipe tobacco because it gave me the most satisfaction.

Unfortunately I had very few shirts, trousers or jackets that didn't have small holes in them caused by chunks of coarse burning tobacco falling on them. But even that couldn't make me give up that devil weed.

In 1973 I gave up for three months after having a heart attack, but I started up again in spite of being told I would be back in hospital if I continued.

Of course, every time I tried to give up almost everyone I came into contact with offered me a cigarette, many of them insisting that I have one, until I gave in.

"That's right," they would say, "one won't do you any harm". But of course it did because once you had one you wanted another and another and so there I was hooked again.

Now, I don't claim any magic cure, nor do I propose to tell you how to stop the habit. But I would like to tell you of the way I was first introduced to that devil weed (do *you* remember your first puff?).

I was eleven when my brother asked me if I had tried a fag. I told him I hadn't, so he said, "Well, you want to try one. We'll pick up some dog ends when we go for a walk with dad on Sunday".

My brother was three years older than me and he had been smoking for some time, not in front of our parents of course, but somewhere across the fields or in an old barn.

Sunday morning came, up the lane we went and along the North Road. My brother pulled hold of my jacket. "Hang back," he said,

The author - fag in hand - in the days when smoking was second nature

"We'll pick up some dog ends".

So there we were tagging along behind and every time we saw a cigarette we would nip down quick and pick it up. I was always afraid our dad would look around at that vital moment, but miraculously he never did.

I don't know if you remember but when cigarette ends were thrown from a car in pre-war days they seemed to go out quickly, leaving quite a bit of tobacco, not like today's filter tips.

Yet another roll-up in a life dedicated to
The Weed

On some of our later walks we would hit the jackpot when someone had emptied a car ashtray and we had enough smokes for a week.

When we got back home from our first Sunday's scavenging and our dad had settled down for a nap, my brother signalled - with a nod and raised eyebrows - for me to go outside.

Up the back garden path we went to the old earth closet which we could hide behind should anyone come.

My brother took some dark shag that he had previously nicked from dad's tobacco tin and mixed it with tobacco from the dog ends. He then rolled up this mixture in an AG cigarette paper which he had also nicked from dad's tin.

I produced a clay bubble pipe from my pocket, one that I often carried around. I would put it into my mouth and suck, pretending to be smoking. After stuffing the bowl full of that foul mixture, I put a match to it and drew in a mouthful, which made me cough and splutter.

"Whatcha doing?" my brother asked, bursting himself laughing.

"Cor, that's awful, I nearly choked myself," I replied. I was, of

89

course, most reluctant to take another puff.

"Come on," said my brother, "take another draw or it'll go out, you'll be all right when you get used to it."

I took another puff, but this once again made me splutter and cough. "I don't know," I said, "I don't think I want to smoke, it's awful".

"That it ain't. Want to be grown up don't you? Well, you gotta learn to smoke."

If this is what it took to be grown up, I would rather not bother, thank you very much, I thought. But to please my brother I continued to keep puffing away at the pipe, only now I was taking very small puffs each time.

My brother finished his roll up and I knocked the remaining tobacco out. "Gotta chew some grass now," said my brother, "so they can't smell the smoke on our breath."

After a while we went back indoors. Before long I began to feel terrible. I rushed outside and had hardly got out of the door when I was violently sick. I thought I would die.

I was never keen to try any more, but my brother was forever goading me and everybody else smoked, so I gradually began to have the odd cigarette.

Fourteen was the age for leaving school at that time and at sixteen you were legally allowed to smoke.

I waited until then but I only bought the odd ten Tenners - do you remember them? They were awful (one packet lasted me the week).

A week after my sixteenth birthday, on March 3, 1939, I put my age forward by one year to join the Territorial Army. It was then that I really began to smoke mainly to mask the pong of that line of latrine buckets.

I have smoked almost everything since then and finally gave up some years ago.

And do you know, I don't miss my smokes one little bit.

- S F Wiles

'Pack up your troubles
in your old kit-bag
And smile, smile, smile!
While you've a lucifer to light your fag,
Smile, boys, that's the style'
So sang the Tommies in World War I...

BACK in those days, the Woodbine was the poor man's smoke; a small cigarette; and five in number were presented in a little green paper packet. Remember?

The Army nickname was 'coffin nails', which indicates that even so far away and long ago their use was suspect.

As schoolboys we were told that smoking was bad for breathing and stunted growth.

However, we revelled in Blue Book; a mixture of all the more exotic cigarettes. And we seldom failed to take a delicate little cigarette called My Darling to dances, to offer to our favourite partners as we sat on the stairs. (These were nearly always refused!)

During the Second World War, I was a prisoner of war in Japan. Our captors gave each man a ration of 40 cigarettes per month, but this was poor consolation to those of us who in the past had opened a new tin of 50 almost as part of the day's routine.

Now was the time for the hoarder and black-marketeer to demand exorbitant sums for even the most inferior brands of tobacco. And so the despised cigarette butt became very precious, particularly when it became known that papers were procurable.

The practice of saving the butt led to class distinctions among smokers.

There were those who continued to treat the butt with contempt, fastidious smokers who were prepared to smoke only their own, those who had no objection to accepting butts handed to them personally by intimate friends, and finally the indiscriminate butt-collecters, one of whom (a top civil servant) was seen searching the ground in the prison's main yard.

This situation was relieved by an issue of Chinese cigarettes. No-one was able to give sensible suggestions as to the composition of

While you've a lucifer to light your fag…
The author and smoking partner light up and pose for the camera

these. When lit, the aroma was reminiscent of stale mutton fat coming strongly through the acrid fumes of a burning joss-stick. Some varieties were perfumed, adding the reek of the cabaret hall to our suffering senses.

The most interesting feature of these cigarettes was the astonishing assortment of designs and trademarks which appeared on the wrappers.

At the sight of them, a number of internees, addicted as much to collecting as to nicotine, glowed with enthusiasm, for here was a great outlet for a suppressed natural instinct.

One man was rumoured to have a collection numbering 180 and another decorated his cell door with pictures cut from the packets.

But for most of us a pretty wrapping was not enough; Chinese cigarettes had a very short run. Their departure was hastened by the arrival of a supply of Japanese tobacco which was usually regarded as cheap and of poor quality but it now displayed hidden virtues.

Finely shredded, but coarse in texture, it became known as Sheikh's Beard. At first we were poor hands at rolling our own but necessity made us expert.

With the help of British cigarette papers we could now enjoy a satisfying smoke.

Unfortunately these papers soon disappeared, and were replaced by a Chinese variety. These were coarse, ungummed and spoilt the flavour of the tobacco. Holding one up to the light, we discovered the watermark of a manufacturer of airmail notepaper.

Our substitute was very much better and far less costly; good quality toilet paper. One sheet could be cut into nine normal-sized cigarette papers.

But this, like so many desirable things, became first scarce then unobtainable. At this stage it began to be rumoured that leaves from the Bible could be bought - at a price!

As we grew accustomed to Sheikh's Beard, the flavour of good tobacco was forgotten.

But not altogether; one night a man came into our cell with a cigarette which had the words Gold Flake printed down the side. It was solemnly passed from hand to hand. We smelt it in turn. Unmistakably, through the smell of mildew, came the faint sweet perfume of genuine Virginia tobacco.

And my most vivid memory of the day of our relief from captivity? The scent of the British tobacco in the pipe of the major who came to our rescue.

The stresses of internment and the cigarette's power to make hunger more bearable undoubtedly contributed to our dependence on nicotine.

- Dr W E Holmes

'The First Cigarette' - an old print

DO YOU REMEMBER?

WHEN you made toast on a fork at the fire?

Marcel waves?

Those balloons, especially the red ones,
that the rag and bone man gave you?

When we all listened to the Saturday night play on the wireless?

Darning our socks?

Hiding from the village bobby on his bike?

When sugar came in blue packets?

Cold bedrooms?

When we walked to school?

Pushing packets of toast down the school radiators
so that they would warm up in time for 'break'?

When lipstick tasted horrible?

The smell when you boiled 'lights' for the cat?

Those two free electric lights that they put in
to encourage us to stop using gaslight?

Rag mats?

Newspaper hanging up behind the door in the outside lavatory?

Your mother taking her 'loaf cake' to the baker's
to be cooked because it wouldn't fit into the new gas oven?

'The Book Club' when you took whatever book they
sent you every month, for 3s. each (15p)?

Short trousers and grazed knees and smelling of TCP?

Sleeping with your grandmother in her deep, feather-filled bed?

When crisps only came in one flavour.
And you could buy them in large tins that the lids never fitted?

The sparks in the wires high above the trolley buses?

The old lady who 'bought' warts?
(They really disappeared didn't they!)

Curling tongs heated on the fire?

Jumping up to close the windows before the train
went into the tunnel, sending the yellow smelly smoke
from the engine into the carriage?

Those fret-saw patterns we used to get every week
in the 'Meccano' magazine?

WHEN Joe Loss played 'In The Mood'
at the Hammersmith Palais?

Your very first ride in a car?

Wearing playform soles?

Icicles in the outside loo?

Eating your first banana when the war was over?

Street teas?

DO YOU REMEMBER?

WHEN it snowed at Christmas.
And holidays were always sunshiny?

Making cushion covers from old black-out material.
And decorating them by winding wool round and round
metal shapes before cutting them out, leaving an untidy tuft
which had to be trimmed?

Pretending you liked that first cigarette?

Carpet squares?

Melamine cups and saucers?

Perms with curlers attached by long wires,
that took hours and hours?

The man on the three-wheeler bicycle who sharpened knives
for 2d each (less than 1p)?

Buying your first plastic mac?

'Pea-souper' fog hanging round the lights in the living room?

- Dorothy Dibb

Happy memories to all Yours readers !